MW00938276

From
Egopreneur
to
Ultrapreneur

By
Nigel D. Clayton

Published 2011 by Ultrapreneur Coach, Denver, Colorado

www.NigelClaytonCoaching.com

E-mail: Nigel@NigelClaytonCoaching.com

All rights reserved. No part of this book may be reproduced or transmitted in any form, or by any means, electronic or mechanical, without written permission from the author, except for the inclusion of brief quotations in a review.

Ultrapreneur® is a trademark owned by Nigel D. Clayton.

Table of Contents

Foreword

During the boom years at the end of the 20th Century, 65 percent of entrepreneurial businesses failed within their first five years. Today that failure rate is 95 percent. Yet, entrepreneurial businesses are started every day. They're considered the backbone of the American economy. We live in a great country; as long as it's legal, you can start whatever kind of business you want here almost immediately. Great ideas as well as not so great ideas become businesses. But the numbers don't lie: Most of them fail. What's not apparent to most people is why.

Do certain people have the magic touch, or do they know something the rest of us don't? This doesn't seem to be the case. For every example of what it takes to be successful, it seems that you can find the contrary. People that have incredible educations seem to fail just as often as those that don't. Some people get rich from selling something that doesn't even seem saleable. When Starbucks started its business, the number of coffee drinkers was down while the price of coffee was going up. In most U.S. cities today, you only need to drive a few blocks before finding a Starbucks. And, despite the jokes about the company's seven-dollar cup of coffee, customers keep coming.

There are hundreds of books on how to be successful, lots of them specifically for the entrepreneurial business owner. So, why do so many fail? Do the business owners not read these books? Do they just not understand what the author is trying to tell them? Are entrepreneurs just stupid? We know this isn't true simply by looking at examples like Google and You

Tube. Not only did the entrepreneurs behind these ventures succeed, but they came up with products so effective that they positively impact the way most of us conduct our day-to-day lives. How did the creative minds that started these businesses succeed so wildly while most others – many of whom are equally talented – fail so miserably? There are seminars galore on how to be successful. There are many people that are willing to coach you to success. If these work, why are the statistics so bad?

Over twenty years ago, I started to look into why entrepreneurial businesses fail so readily. I feel like I tried almost everything that came along the pike. I read this book and that book; I went to this seminar and that seminar. I asked everyone that I could talk to. I talked with successful entrepreneurs and unsuccessful entrepreneurs. I talked with bankers, financial planners, attorneys... you name it, and I've talked to them. I came up with no answers that were universal.

This book is about how I came up with the answers for myself. I am a successful entrepreneur. I have owned one of my businesses for almost 25 years, and several years ago I started a second business, soon followed by a third business. I love what I do all day long and my businesses continue to grow every year. I found the secret to my success.

In this book, I will take you through the trials and tribulations of the start-up entrepreneurial business. I will also tell you my story. Then I will introduce you to the most critical step in achieving entrepreneurial success: finding your *authentic self*. This is the golden thread that should ideally run through everything you do. I'll guide you to actions that lead you closer to your authentic self, and each time you move in this direction, your confidence will grow by such leaps that soon you won't imagine being anything else but authentic. By using what comes naturally to you, the professional or personal obstacles that once caused you so much pain won't seem like obstacles at all. Once you gain confidence – which happens quickly – you'll see how resoundingly simple this plan is.

I'll show you how to connect the crucial thread of authenticity through the next four steps to the entrepreneurial high road. Going through this process will eventually help you to see things differently: that the ultimate reward of success in business is not money but *freedom* – freedom to spend your time and conduct your life as you choose.

At the end of this book, you'll find information on continuing this entrepreneurial evolution through highly effective, tailor-made coaching sessions with me where I help you to quickly zero in on the obstacles that are impeding your happiness and freedom. I also include worksheets to help you examine where you currently are on the journey to success. As you go through my coaching process, you will find yourself quickly growing from Egopreneur to Ultrapreneur® – and achieving a quality of life that you'd never imagined could be yours.

This journey is a wonderful circle that brings you back to a greater version of your authentic self each time. And, best of all, it won't seem like work. You will simply be what you are meant to be. As a result, you'll do what other successful businesses owners do: only what you love and nothing else.

Authentic Self

confidence

Awareness

Freedom
Success

Systems — Time

Ego-preneur
Entre-preneur
ultra-preneur

Vision

comfort
Zones

The Typical Entrepreneurial Beginning...
The Egopreneur

I* decided to start my own business after being laid off several times in a few years and my prospects for new jobs became fewer and fewer. I took the plunge. After all, I had been the manager of my department, an executive in control of people and money, and had earned increasing responsibilities – that is, until my industry took a turn south.

Even so, I was a manager, a problem solver and someone people had looked up to for guidance. And before I made the decision to start my own business, I had done my research. I had also shared my vision with my family, some of whom gave me the all-inspiring, "Are you nuts? What are you thinking?" and others who genuinely encouraged me, "Follow your dreams."

So, with no clear-cut answer from my family, I spoke to friends and colleagues. These opinions were equally split, although the answers tended to lean toward the practical, "Of course, follow your dreams. But, have a backup plan in case it doesn't work out."

The more I asked, the more I did not get a clear answer. So, being the manager I am, I researched other avenues. I spoke to the local Chamber of Commerce, the Small Business Administration and other small business owners. Again, the more I researched, the cloudier the answers seemed to be.

I heard that having a business of your own is not all it's

---

* The "I" in this chapter is not actually me, but rather a hypothetical person who becomes an entrepreneur.

1

cracked up to be. Long hours, no time off. But, nobody tells you what to do. Is that good or bad, or both? I wasn't sure. I felt schizophrenic. It's good. It's bad. I don't know.

To further my investigation, I did the inevitable: I created a business plan. I spent enormous amounts of time on this business plan, this business bible. For, while I had been a manager, I had not been a marketer, accountant or visionary. I had to think of an enterprise that did not exist yet and imagine it to the *nth* degree.

I also had to distinguish myself from the crowd. It seemed like everyone was trying to go into business for themselves now, and competition was fierce. It wasn't just on my own turf; with the rapid growth of the Internet, the competition was quickly becoming global. When I went to the Chamber of Commerce leads group to find some initial customers, people were asking me, "Why should I buy from you? How are you different?" I had to look inside myself and ask, well, how am I different? When I worked as a manager in corporate America, the thing I loved the most, and was the best at, was finding new, innovative ideas for how to make things work. So, that's the approach I took with my clients, and they really responded to it.

Then I agonized over my cash flow projections. Were they too conservative? Too optimistic? Or, were they off the mark altogether? I had an army of people review my business plan: family, friends and people at the Chamber of Commerce. At some point, it seemed as though I would need to scrap the whole thing and start all over again. But, after bearing my soul for what seemed like an eternity, I arrived at a satisfying stopping point. Or, perhaps I was just tired of thinking about. Anyway, I decided to go with it. I got approval for a line of credit and was ready to start my new life.

I was determined to be successful. I listened to motivation tapes when I got discouraged and kept telling myself I was going to be one of the ones that made it. After all, the bank believed in me enough to provide a line of credit, didn't they? No, this was going to work. I had a great plan, a worthwhile product to sell. The market was there. I had even contracted the services of a friend who knew something about Web design, and was ready to start taking orders on my company's new site. I was going to be a success. I was on the road to being an entrepreneur, to creating my own destiny. Nobody would stop me with the glass ceiling again.

But, in the back of my mind, I kept thinking, *I wonder what I don't know. What's out there that is going to stop me?*

I opened my business. I never thought I could experience the amount of adrenalin that I did that day. It was fantastic. It was so uplifting. Everyone I came in contact with was helpful, positive and wished me the best. The entire day went superbly. It was going to happen: I was going to be a success. Being an entrepreneur was exhilarating. I did not come down from this adrenalin high for weeks.

The next several weeks... Oh, the next several weeks, I was legit, a true entrepreneur. I was selling my product to people who needed and valued it. I was getting orders through my Web site, too. Not as many as I was eventually hoping to get, but a solid start nonetheless. As word spread about my business, my Web hits would no doubt increase, as would the number of my actual online customers. At least, that's what I thought. This sales thing was trickier than I imagined it would be. At first, I counted on orders from people that I already knew: former clients, friends and even family. Eventually, through persistent networking and clever marketing (with the help of another friend who was savvy in this area), my customer base and orders steadily grew, but they were certainly hard won. Overall, I felt like my sales were good, especially when I heard that many of my competitors weren't selling enough to make ends meet and were even going out of business. I felt like I had beaten the odds. Why hadn't I gone into business for myself the first time I was laid off? I would be further ahead by now. Oh well, I was on my way.

After the first several months – those exhilarating months where everything felt right – I became busy enough that I had trouble setting aside enough time to invoice my customers. Oh well, I'll do that later, I thought. After all, this was wonderful. I was too busy selling, and I had a line of credit, so I kept selling. It will all work out. It has to, doesn't it? When I wasn't selling, I was marketing to fill the funnel for future sales, and ordering to fill current sales.

My life was like a whirlwind, exciting and fulfilling. In fact, as the months went by, I was so busy selling and ordering, I was spending less time marketing. Around the sixth month that I was in business, I decided that I didn't need to market anymore. My Webmaster friend had set up a good site for me. I didn't need to be tech savvy; he'd taken care of all of that, and customers would be sure to find me on the Internet now. I had enough business and I had more in the pipeline. My days were filled with helping my customers. I had little time for my family and none for my friends.

Every month I was selling a little more. I felt such energy and validation. I was getting referrals from existing customers. At this rate, I would perhaps reach my business plan goals sooner than I thought. I was so busy I didn't return all the calls I received. Even though customers could communicate with me through e-mail and the contact form on my Web site, it still seemed that what they often wanted was to actually speak to a person. I wrote down the voice mail messages and promised myself I would call them later, as soon as I got the next order out. Days, weeks and months went by. Then, things started to change.

Not only was I unable to keep up with orders, but I couldn't keep up with anything that needed to get done. I was struggling to find enough time to have a discussion with my Webmaster about my site's search engine, which apparently wasn't optimized. My monthly hits weren't what I'd imagined they'd be. Some of my customers were also complaining that my Web site was difficult to use. I wasn't expecting this. A redesign was in order, but when would this happen? I wasn't paying my bills on time. I wasn't ordering on time to supply my customers. I wasn't making deposits, and I was overdrawing my bank account. How do I get out of this?

Of course, I told myself, I need help. First, I'll hire a virtual assistant to help answer e-mails and to answer customers' questions during peak Web traffic hours in an online chat room on my company Web site. We'd be providing customers with the information they wanted, instantaneously and right at their fingertips. I was no tech genius, but I was proud of myself for thinking of adding this feature. Why hadn't I thought of this sooner?

I'll also hire Nancy, a friend of mine who'd been bugging me for months to let her work with me, to help in my office. That's it. Whew. Problems solved. I just needed to use those executive skills. I talked to Nancy the next day and let her know that her job with me would be temporary and part-time at first, but once things got straightened out, I could hire her as a permanent, full-time employee.

So, Nancy and my virtual assistant came on board. The virtual assistant got right to the task, and soon reported that he was chatting online with a variety of customers – existing and potential – every day. It was such a relief to know that my Internet communications were in good hands. Nancy, too, immediately helped to lift my burdens. I had her do things while I did other things. I would now be able to get twice as much done and, before long, this nightmare would be under control.

The first week was great. I was no longer fighting this battle alone. I had allies; I had people to take some of the pressure off me. For the next several weeks, we rode out to battle together on a daily basis. We were putting out fires left and right. We were a team destined to conquer any situations that would arise, and go home at the end of each day victorious. Why hadn't I done this earlier?

I had six weeks of bliss. Then, things started to change – *again*. Oh, the phone kept ringing, but most of the calls were from vendors I had not paid, not from customers. What was happening? This has to be a fluke. What did I do to upset my customers? They weren't calling.

Again, my executive skills came into play. I was a creative problem solver, after all. Of course, I had stopped marketing because I was so busy filling customers' orders. All I had to do was contact the customers and things would be right again. I also left a message with my Webmaster, telling him to get started on a new, more customer-friendly design for my Web site. The doubt that had come over me was now easy to dismiss as being that of someone without my background and skills, but not me.

But, wait a minute; should I go out and market or should I send Nancy? Well, if I send Nancy, I could get the orders filled, talk to customers when they called, catch up on adminis-trative work as well as place orders with vendors, and gener-ally get in control.

"Nancy," I said, "Go out to our existing customers and drum

up some business while I hold down the fort." *Off she went. This is great!* Now I could smooth things out and this wouldn't happen again. *I am so the entrepreneur.* Just a speed bump: I can overcome this.

Nancy was gone for a week, then two. I had begun to catch up on a lot of things while she was gone. I could see the surface of my desk for the first time in months. I had neat little piles of paper. I was getting organized. But, after two weeks, Nancy had come up with very little new business. "They're all fine," she told me. "They don't need anything right now, but they'll get in touch with us as soon as they do."

Fear and doubt came rushing in again. "Well," I said to Nancy, putting on my entrepreneur's hat and thinking positively again, "if that's the case, we'll just have to find new customers."

I sent Nancy to the Chamber of Commerce leads group, thinking that in no time she'd generate new customers. After all, the leads group knew my company, and Nancy is great with people. *Problem solved. It's all about problem solving.* But, after she had been attending the group for several weeks and yielded no results, I began to worry again. Ugh. A month had gone by and there was nothing filling the funnel. *This isn't working.*

Fortunately, I was still getting money from serving customers in the past, and especially because I was able to send out billings last month. But, what was I going to do next month?

I was getting tired.

Wait a minute; I had been doing this all wrong. *I'll go out and market. I'm the one who brought in the business before. It's not that there's no business; it's that the wrong person has been doing the marketing.* I'll go out and market and have Nancy fill customers' orders, place orders with vendors and answer the phone. I can even train her how to do the dreaded administrative and accounting work. Yes, that's the ticket. Problem solved. It's all about problem solving.

I got back on the marketing trail. First, I decided to visit my existing customers. Initially it was slow going, but by the end of the week I had new business, including one customer who represented a significant order. My instincts were proving to be right on target.

I continued contacting my existing customers the following week and again, I had new business by the end of the week. I was beginning to feel good.

In the early mornings and late afternoons, I spent time touching base with my virtual assistant and instructing Nancy about the tasks I wanted her to complete besides answering the phones and filling the orders: that administrative stuff that I wanted off my plate. Each day, I diligently asked them if they had completed the assigned tasks from the day before. "Yes," they both told me, "all done." This was terrific. I was now able to spend most of my time prospecting new business, and the other tasks that were dull and boring, but necessary, were being completed at the same time by other people. Again, why hadn't I done this before? Oh well, now everything would work out.

Business continued to come in and I was feeling enthusiastic. Everything got better and better, but only for a while. Gears began to shift yet again. I had gotten new business. I had given my assistants the information. Orders were filled, but not exactly: They weren't being filled on a timely basis, and they were often incomplete. Vendors were not getting paid on time, so they weren't shipping us the product to sell. Customers weren't getting billed until a considerable amount of time after the order had been filled.

I was back at square one. On top of that, I discovered that

Nancy had not been pleasant and professional to some of the customers. I also learned that my virtual assistant had left several important e-mails unanswered and had been less than helpful to many customers who visited my site's chat room. Some of these customers even interpreted his responses to them as terse. After getting angry with myself, angry with my assistants, confused and scared, and talking to friends and family, I decided to let Nancy as well as my virtual assistant go. I didn't want to. It meant I was going to have to do every-thing myself again. But, everything was so messed up that I didn't know where else to start.

Even if I decided to keep my assistants, it would take more time for me to straighten them out than if I just did the work myself. Above and beyond that, I had the fear of losing customers. How could my hired help have done this to me – especially Nancy? After all, she was a friend. She knew how much this business meant to me. She was there when I initially started talking about it. She had really disappointed me. Not only had she failed to produce sales with existing customers when I had somehow been able to, but she had really made a mess of all the other things I had left her in charge of.

I might as well do it myself.

My previous words kept haunting me: *I wonder what I don't know, and what is out there that's going to stop me?* Well, what I *did* know 18 months after I started my business was that I hadn't known a lot. Sure, I had started my own company and I was selling my own product, and was on the map. But, I was working long hours six and seven days a week. I had no time.

I spent all my time at work. I was marketing and going to leads groups, going to marketing functions, talking to this person, talking to that person. I was trying to pay attention to my

Web site. I was hoping to order enough supplies, but not too much – hoping I would make the sales before I had to pay the bills. And then there were the endless administrative tasks, and worst of all, the accounting. My life was hell.

I had not gone beyond my sales peak for over eight months, just enough to get by, but having to use all my credit and even borrowing some money from my family – the worst thing I had to do since opening my doors. It was only temporary, I told them, a glitch in ordering. I tried to convince them – and myself – that I wasn't in any trouble and was confident in my success.

The truth was that I was so busy being busy, doing everything, that I wasn't sure where I really was. I didn't know if I would be a success or out of business within a short time. Help! How do I get out of this? What had I done wrong? Looking back, it didn't seem I had done anything wrong. In fact, at the time, I was sure I had done everything right.

Nobody but an entrepreneur could understand what I was going through and what I needed. That's it; that's it! Nancy and my virtual assistant didn't work out because they weren't entrepreneurs. They were employees. What I needed was a partner, someone that saw things the way I saw them. Someone who tackled business with the same sense of urgency that I did. After we got going, then we could hire employees again. We needed to get the basics under control first.

The idea of a partner came to me so quickly, I think, because John, a person I had met in my Chamber leads group, and I had always clicked. We'd had several conversations in the past, all of them positive and rewarding. I felt he really understood what I was talking about. We were on the same page. We seemed to get excited about the same things at the same time. That's who I need – John. We had even jokingly said that we should be in business together. The more I thought about it, the more I said to myself, yes, why not?

I approached John. We had a great meeting. I left feeling quite jazzed. My enthusiasm returned, and I was excited about what we could do together. We had several more meetings and after each one, I felt better and better. He really did understand. We saw eye to eye. It was really exciting to talk with someone about how I viewed things and to see him immediately comprehend my vision. The really great thing about this was that John already had his own business and it complemented mine.

This was terrific. We could cross-sell to each other's customers. We'd grow twice as fast. I'd finally be going in the right direction to be successful. I could put all the things that hadn't worked behind me.

Well, it's behind me alright – including my partnership with John, which failed within a few months. I haven't even been in business for two years yet, and I'm exhausted, overworked, overwhelmed, underpaid, scared and generally miserable. I'm wondering how I can get out of this mess with my self respect.

Author's note: This is an example of a typical entrepreneurial beginning that I have observed over and over again. The trials and tribulations may include different specific circumstances for different business owners, but the results are usually the same. After several years of dealing with unforeseen situations, the business owners I've talked to feel just as depleted and frightened as the entrepreneur in the example you just read. This is a terrible place to be and strikes at the heart of entrepreneurs' self worth. They begin to doubt themselves and whether their businesses will survive. They have invested so much – financially, emotionally and especially their time. I find this situation to be true of companies that have been in business for even 10 or 20 years; the owners still feel they are, at best, surviving. They still work long hours six and seven days a week. They feel they're not moving forward fast enough, and sometimes, not at all.

Why does this happen? Is it a matter of the business owner not having enough capital, not enough business training, the right employees or the right partners? Again, for every reason you can come up with, you can also find the contrary to be true in other business ventures. So, what is it?

My Story

I was born Nigel David Skipton of English parents in a small town in Northhamptonshire, England. The population was 40,000 people and the predominant industries were shoe factories and farming. I don't remember very much of my early years. However, I do remember going to English public school, wearing a uniform, ink wells in the desks and head-masters with long canes ready to swat you on the knuckles if you did anything wrong. The school system was very structured, strict and conservative, with punishment ready to be handed out at the slightest hint of disobedience. The society in general in my hometown was the same: very serious, with a right and wrong way to do everything.

I do remember it being cold. We did not have central heating. One room in the house had a coal fireplace and we would huddle there to keep warm. We would put hot water bottles under our bed covers about 15 minutes before retiring for the night to take the freezing chill off the sheets. I also remember we had a car that had to be cranked to start it. You'd insert the crank in a slot on the outside front of the car, which proved difficult and frustrating to my father when it was cold outside. This is what I remember of England in the 1950s. In my hometown, the average winter temperature was 46 degrees F, and the average summer temperature was 64 degrees F.

This all changed when I turned seven. A lot of things changed. First, my name changed from Skipton to Clayton, or so I thought. When I asked my mother, "Didn't I used to be called Skipton?" she said no! For a long time I thought I was a little crazy. I could have sworn my name was Skipton. I remembered using it in school, hadn't I? Another thing that changed...we moved to the United States. We moved in July to southern New Mexico where the average summer temperature was much more than 64 degrees. We now lived in the desert where it was in the 100s. I no longer wore a uniform to school, but was given a flat top haircut, a tee-shirt, and jeans. No longer did I have headmasters in black robes with long canes attached to them. Now the teachers had big paddles with holes in them. I was paddled for not checking my math home-work, even though I knew it was all correct. Nevertheless, the mood at the Air Force base school system I attended was less serious and more nurturing than the public schools in England had been. There were definite ideas as to what was right and wrong, but society here was at least willing to sometimes look at things in new ways.

It was the time of Elvis Presley, a growing economy, hope and optimism. I felt free to express myself. I became an extro-vert with a great sense of humor. The other kids called me Moon Man because, they said, my humor was so out of this world. I also discovered that I liked helping others. However, my teachers didn't seem to agree that this was something I should do. On my third grade report card I received a "C" in conduct. In the comments section of the report card my teacher wrote..."Nigel's grades would be even better if he wasn't spending so much time helping others." I remember getting in trouble for that, and being told to stop helping others.

In New Mexico, I also realized class distinction for the first time. Most of the kids I became friends with were officers' children. My father was not an officer. Even though we had all colors of people from many, many countries working on the Air Force base, the prejudice was of rank. I could not swim in the officer's swimming pool with my friends. I had to swim in the non-commissioned officer's (NCO) pool.

After three years in New Mexico we moved back to England. It was a great time to be there. It was the '60s, and England was the world leader in music and fashion: the Beatles, the Stones and the mod scene. Again, I went to the U.S. Air Force base schools. We lived in my hometown and on each school day we rode a bus 30 miles to the base. I began to feel a change in myself. I was no longer the outgoing, humorous, fun-loving person I had been. Part of it was being a teenager, but there was more to it than that. I began to feel a separation.

I was separated from the kids I went to school with because I lived so far away from the base, and the only friends I played with were the English kids I knew in my hometown. My mother felt uncomfortable about inviting anyone from the base schools home because we had no indoor toilets, no central heating, and we had to bring a metal tub into the kitchen in order to take a bath. I didn't think much of it until I couldn't invite people home. Then I began to feel inadequate, different, and simply not cool enough. This was the beginning of me turning inward, being more of an introvert.

At that same time, my father and I became distant. He was very serious and it was easier for me to be an introvert around him. He worked as a mechanic for the Air Force, mostly working on heavy machines. He was a very literal guy; to him, if he couldn't see it or touch it, it didn't exist. The more I went inward, the more I began to read. I always had my nose in a book. My father interpreted this as me having my head in the clouds and this did not endear me to him. My brother, on the other hand, who was happy to work with him on the week-ends fixing something under a greasy car, had a much closer relationship. Auto mechanics did not appeal to me at all and I did everything I could to avoid even the possibility of doing such work.

However, I really did enjoy my time in England in the '60s. With my English class, I went to see Shakespeare's *Hamlet* in Stratford-upon-Avon, which I liked immensely. My English teacher, Mrs. Killabrew, was great. She was very encouraging to me. She seemed to see through all those things that separated me from others and made me feel inadequate – to see the true me. She could see my worth, unlike others. I also enjoyed all the great music and fashion and the long summer days. During the summer, I was a coxman for the local town rowing team: I was responsible for steering the boat as eight men rowed as hard as they could. This was a great feeling of importance and recognition.

But, by the time we moved back to the United States for a second time in late 1967, I felt more and more isolated. This time my father was stationed at a base in Illinois. Again, we lived many miles from the school and from any kids who went there. I remember the fashion was different than it had been in England – not as cutting edge. The town was very conservative and there were farms all around. I did not feel comfortable and did not feel like I fit in. Even the kids in the school were different. There was a combination of base school children and farmers' children. I not only felt the difference of the farm kids but the separation from the base kids. Maybe it was because of my past experiences with class prejudice. I spent most of my time reading in the library and in my room. I was a complete introvert. And then something miraculous happened.

After being in Illinois for only a few months, my father was diagnosed with leukemia so we moved to San Antonio where the big Air Force hospital was located. We went from a very cold winter climate to the warm desert. This wasn't the only thing that was warm. It was amazing. The things that made me feel separated, inadequate, and led me to become more and more introverted in recent years were prized in Texas. Because I still had an English accent and the TV show "The Monkees" was popular, the Texas girls loved me. The fact that I was shy and liked music, fashion, poetry, plays and so forth was even better. Again, I had to ride a bus to school, but this time it was to my advantage. The people that rode the bus with me were most of the football team. Believe it or not, they liked me, mostly because I knew so many of the girls. It was the best of both worlds; both the big men on campus liked me as well as the girls, even the good looking ones. This was the best year of my life.

I had a great time in Texas, but after a year we moved again, this time to Los Angeles. By now my accent had faded, and in California I was no longer friends with the football players and the girls seemed to show me no interest. It was as though I had gone back in time to when I left England. I felt out of place and scared. The kids in L.A. were mean; there were gangs, and students were getting stabbed and killed. Every-thing was so much more crowded, smoggy, and fast paced, with no sense of community like there had been in Texas. I stuck very close to home and retreated to my room. What had happened; why couldn't we have stayed in Texas?

A year after moving to Los Angeles, my father died, except, as I found out, he was actually my stepfather. My real father's name was Skipton. I was not crazy after all. My mother said she didn't know how to tell me at the time. We moved to Tucson, Arizona. I finished the last two years of high school in Tucson. However, most of the people I went to high school with in Tucson knew me by my middle name, David. Because I had moved so much before, I had been introduced to my classes as a new student many times. Most of the teachers could not pronounce Nigel correctly. This usually caused a round of laughter from my fellow students – another reason I felt out of place, separated, and inadequate. But, I thought, everyone could pronounce David. It worked, so I used it. I felt like I fit in more, and by the time I left high school I had friends, girlfriends, and felt more complete. Things had turned around, but not to the point they were in Texas, though. I was not as extroverted, confident, or popular, but things were definitely better.

Then I entered the University of Arizona – barely. Because I had gone to six different high schools in two different countries and four different states, my grades were not stellar. So I just squeaked past the office of admissions; but I made it. Figuring out my major was a much more difficult task. Because of all the high schools I had attended, science was not something I was able to pursue; I was never able to catch up with all the lab work required. I was good at reading and math, so I decided I would become a lawyer. But, after several years of taking a lot of political science, I met several law school graduates that couldn't get a job other than bartending. Deciding this was a lot of work to become a bartender, I changed my major. I had thought about becoming a philosophy professor, because I really enjoyed this subject and had gone drinking with a few of my professors. This is a great job, I thought: They spend all day talking philosophy and then they spend the summers in Cancun, Mexico, drinking on the beach. But, I also met a lot of people that had PhDs in philosophy that couldn't find jobs either. I know, I thought, I'll become an architect. Architects make money; they drive Porsches; and there are job openings for architects. After making four Ds and an F my first semester in architectural school, I decided this was not meant to be.

I went to a school counselor to help me decide what to do next. He asked me what my best subject was. I told him math.

He said to become an accountant. So I did. I had no idea what an accountant was when I decide to become one. I just knew it had something to do with math. Math had always been easy for me. I used to finish my math homework in class. This was how I was able to catch up with things so fast while moving so much during high school...math was easy and I loved to read. By the time I started taking accounting classes I was again very much an introvert. The college life had also made me go within. There were many different groups in college. There were the fraternities, the war protestors, ROTC, religious groups, and groups according to your major. The fraternities didn't appeal to me. They reminded me of the meanness I had encountered in Los Angeles. I wasn't interested in protesting, although I didn't want to go to war either. I felt the religious groups were always trying to convince everyone else that their way was the only way. Why if they were so sure did they find it necessary to convert everyone else? Since most people taking my major of accounting were in fraternities, I again felt I was on the outside.

After six years, I finally graduated. The time was the mid-70s. I had a beard and hair that wasn't really long, but not short either. All the big CPA firms at the time wanted their employees to look very conservative...no facial hair and very short hair with grey or dark blue suits. They looked like dorks. Not wanting to look like a dork, I decided the big CPA firms were not for me...I would work for a small, local company. I signed up to interview at the University with some local accounting companies. One company looked very interesting, but I couldn't find any information on it before I went into my interview. However, it was a small, local company and this was what I was looking for. I had worn a tie to my interview but no suit jacket; it was 110 degrees outside. The interviewer asked me if I knew anything about the company. I told him there were no brochures left, so I didn't know anything about the company other than it was local. He proceeded to show me a map of the world that had dots all over it. "These dots show where we are located throughout the world," he said. Then he told me, "We are the largest CPA firm in the world." Wow, so much for interviewing with a small local company. Needless to say, I wasn't hired.

In fact, I couldn't find a job at all. After many months, the only job I could find was working for the university in the Grants Department. It was a very boring job. It was not stimulating or challenging. Great, I had worked my ass off for the last several years, taking a lot of credit hours to graduate and trying to make ends meet with part time jobs as a janitor, a vacuum cleaner salesman, a rent-a-cop, and a night clerk for several hotels, only to get a job that doesn't pay very well and is boring. I got married.

My wife's father offered me a job in his family-owned business in Colorado. After a year of working in the family business it became apparent that it could only support one family; both of my brother-in-laws and I were working in the business. So, I left to work for a small community college in the mountains. Finally, I was employed in my profession; I was the accountant for the college - its only accountant - and was making good money as well as living in the beautiful Rocky Mountains. I was expecting my second child and life was good. Two months after I started the job a new college president was hired. He fired the person that hired me and was supposedly going to mentor me. Instead, for the next six months I received no support, with the idea that when the independent audit was performed things would be so bad that my new boss could fire me easily. So much for life being good. I had just quit the family business hoping to prove to my father-in-law that I could make it on my own, was expecting my second child, and my boss was hoping to fire me.

I worked my ass off for the next six months. I studied all of my college accounting books again, making sure I wouldn't miss anything that the audit might uncover. I worked weekends going over the work that the four accounting clerks were supposed to do, but having no allegiance to me, I wasn't sure I could trust anything they did. I was under immense pressure to succeed. The audit came...I had no idea how things would turn out. I'll never forget the meeting with the auditors and the president to review the findings of the audit. The president asked the head auditor how the audit went. The auditor exclaimed, "This is the cleanest the books have been in years!" The president said, "Thank you," and walked out of the room. I passed the ordeal. I beat them. What a relief. I left soon after to move back to Denver, as my wife wanted to be closer to her family.

The next couple of years I spent working for a county government – which was like being on the set of The Exorcist – and various real estate development companies, until the real estate market crashed and I was out of work. In that time I had lost one of my daughters to a freak accident and had gotten divorced soon after that. I had no job, no savings, and no family.

I decided to start my own bookkeeping service after working for one for several months, with the intent being that this would give me free time to discover what I really wanted to be when I grew up, as accounting had not been very successful. What I discovered was that having my own business and having direct contact with the clients was the piece that had been missing when I had worked as an accountant for other companies. I felt that I had real impact on whether they were going to be successful by helping my clients understand what their financial statements were saying about their business.

I worked seven days a week and as many hours a day as I could stay awake. After several months I began to wonder if starting my own business had been the right thing. After all, what made me think I could be successful myself? I had never worked for myself before. What was I thinking? I felt like I was back at the community college again – under the gun. I had already taken several steps backward by working as a bookkeeper for a bookkeeping company; after all, I had been a controller for a real estate development company. But now everything was at stake. My resume was not looking like the picture of someone that was continually moving up the ladder. I had not only gone backwards, but had been unemployed several times in the last several years. I had to make it...I had to.

That was over 25 years ago. Since then I have been running my own CPA firm, specializing in working with entrepreneurial business owners. Several years ago I started my second company, a professional business coaching company, also working with entrepreneurial business owners. Yes, I made it.

The last two and a half decades have not been easy. I almost went out of business several times and had to borrow money several times to keep the business going. I went through what most entrepreneurial business owners go through: the ups and downs of owning your own business. I was married and divorced again. I became a partner in a CPA firm and then was forced to leave the partnership. I got so depressed; I just wanted to escape from everything. I almost gave up a million times. But, I didn't. The last 25 years have been my journey of discovering what it takes to be a successful entrepreneurial business owner.

When I started my business, I thought that all I needed to do in order to ensure my clients' success was to give them accurate and up-to-date financial statements. I was like most accountants. I told my clients, "Here are your current financial statements. If you have any questions, give me a call." I soon discovered that this was not the secret to the small business owner's success. First of all, they didn't know the questions to ask because most of them didn't understand their financial statements. As soon as I came to this realization, I decided I had to look at things differently. Instead of looking at myself as the service provider of my clients, I began to look at what would make me successful. After all, I was in the same boat. I was an entrepreneur that wanted to be successful also. The more I could understand what I needed to do to be successful, the more I could help my clients. And the more I could help them become successful, the more successful I would be.

As a new small-business owner, I did everything, much like most entrepreneurs do. I was excited, scared, and involved with every aspect of the business. I had to be; I was the only one in the business. As I mentioned before, I worked many hours a day and every day of the week. At first, when you're so afraid that you will not succeed, you have adrenaline that keeps you going. This kept me going for the first couple of years, especially with the revenues increasing. I must be doing something right...right? After seven years, I wasn't so sure. Yes, I had been in business for seven years. I had not failed, but I was exhausted. I was still working seven days a week and 10-plus hours a day. I did not have a life outside of my business. I had hit a ceiling for what I could do by myself with my business. This was a turning point for me in understanding what it takes to be a successful business owner.

Before hitting that ceiling I thought I had already found the secret through what I had learned while helping my clients up to this point. I had seen that when I visited my clients' businesses, many times I would leave feeling like I had been drinking extra strong coffee at Starbucks all day. The atmosphere was so disorganized and chaotic; it made me feel jittery all over. I discovered that most of the time this meant that the systems in place were too inadequate for the client's company to run smoothly. Despite my overtaxed nerves, I was able to detect what parts of the existing systems were inadequate or what new systems needed to be implemented. When I implemented the right systems for my clients, I helped my company's revenues grow. Drawing on my public accounting auditing experience, most of the systems I put in place were financially related.

I had also gained crucial business expertise during the several years I had spent working for a certified public accounting firm auditing Housing and Urban Development (HUD) low-income housing authorities and American Indian reservations throughout the United States. This work was important because it gave me the skills to understand how financial systems related to all aspects of a business. Also, because we usually didn't have the time typically required to complete audits properly, I had to learn how to be very efficient in detecting weaknesses in the systems and where errors might occur because of those weaknesses. Initially, I thought this was the secret to business success, but when I hit the ceiling for myself, I knew there had to be something more. Although I had implemented effective systems in my own business, I was still working my ass off. I talked with other business owners, business associates, clients, and others to find out how they had broken through this ceiling. All I had to do was ask...right?

Unfortunately, there were no consistent answers. Some had borrowed money to get to the next level. Some had formed partnerships with others. Some just had good luck. There seemed to be no clear answer, although all of them thought they had the right answer. I was feeling trapped. I didn't have enough business to be able to hire another person and didn't have the means to borrow the money required to hire someone, either. What could I do?

In the meantime I was getting more and more exhausted. I had no time to spare. Between picking up my clients' information and delivering their financial statements, inputting all the information into the computer, answering the telephone all day long, billing and collecting, performing the marketing and sales functions, I was swamped. I was also feeling more and more isolated. Even though I knew others had gone through this and had triumphed, I hadn't yet made it through, and I not only felt scared I would fail but I also felt like a fake. How could I help others if I could not do it myself?

This dilemma went on for years, and in that time I became more and more introverted. Oh, I talked with clients and continued to perform the functions that required social interaction, but I was feeling more and more isolated. Since this had been going on for so long, how could I tell anyone? They'd all know I was a fraud. I just kept working harder and harder, and longer and longer hours. To complicate matters, my wife at the time was pressuring me to take my business outside the home and wanted me to make more money. I wanted those things too, but the added pressure just made me feel even more inadequate. I started to look at my time. I decided that – just like when I was auditing – I had to become more efficient. I kept asking myself, *what can I do to get more time?* I was able to come up with some things, but after almost six months I came to the horrible conclusion that they didn't make that much of a difference. I was doomed.

Then a miracle happened. Someone that had hired me years ago to work for one of his clients asked me to join his CPA firm. I would become one of three partners. I would be able to stop doing everything I was currently doing and have the accounting staff do most of it. My time would be filled with preparing more complicated tax returns, which appealed to me. I wanted to be able to show people that I had advanced skills worth charging more than I had ever changed before, and I would also spend much of my time performing marketing and sales functions for the company. This was great. All my problems were solved. I was going to be able to take the business out of home, make more money, and work less. I was not a fraud after all.

A little more than two years later, I was miserable even though I was not only reaching my goals but exceeding them. I was bringing in new business far beyond my expectations. I had turned over all of the menial work to the accounting staff and had implemented a system to share the work more efficiently between them. I was also preparing more complicated tax returns. My skills were improving and I was able to charge more for my services. Everything I wanted to accomplish was happening, but I was miserable. I must be having a mid-life crisis, I told myself. Next I'll want to buy a sports car. The more I stayed with the partnership, the more I became unhappy. A few years later I was asked to leave the partnership, so I did.

I was able to take my client base with me, so I was still in business. But I felt like I was back where I had been before I joined the partnership. I was now back to having survival adrenaline force me through my day. At this point, it had been twelve years since I had decided to go out on my own. I still hadn't made it and was extremely unhappy. I had lost my partnership and my second marriage. I felt like a failure. What I discovered in the ten years that followed this crisis is the secret of my success. It is also the secret of success for any entrepreneurial business owner.

Finding Your Authentic Self

Discovering who you are and what you want to do with your life doesn't always come easy. When I looked at my own life and wrote down my story, it seemed to have no rhyme or reason. To some degree, it looked like I had spent much of my life feeling like I didn't fit in. But these experiences of feeling disconnected actually helped me find my *authentic self*. When I became more introverted, this gave me time to explore myself and find what was truly valuable to me. This has translated into my businesses, which continues to evolve as I create things my way. Everything that you love to do – in your business and in life – stems from your authenticity.

The *authentic self* is how you would be in the world if you were able to shed all the baggage you have accumulated throughout your life by being assimilated into the Borg, if you will. Those of you who are *Star Trek* fans know what the Borg is: a big box that traveled throughout the universe with the sole purpose of assimilating everyone into it so that there was no personal individuality. It was said to be futile to resist the Borg. Consider the saying, "Think outside the box"; the "box" is the Borg.

Being authentic is also how you would actively pursue your passions in life. It's being exactly who you are, and this might mean expanding beyond the confines of the box that society tells us to stay safely within. When you're being authentic, you're completely exposing yourself to the world as *here I am*.

It's not about being rebellious, but it can feel uncomfortable, even frightening to many people because they've been programmed from a young age to do things a certain way and that it's unsafe to veer from the prescribed course. So the typical person tiptoes around his or her authenticity, sometimes embracing it in secret, but mostly hiding it from the world at large. The fact is, when you are being authentic, the world at large usually doesn't notice the difference. My clients are always pleasantly surprised when, after they decide to "step out", nothing catastrophic happens. What does happen is that other people are subconsciously drawn to the confidence and personal power that the authentic you exudes. Your authentic self is you at your best, operating at full potential and fully energized. It's from this point that your business will take off – with surprisingly little effort on your part.

Finding your authentic self starts with taking a long, hard look at yourself – the good, the bad and the ugly. It's about accepting and appreciating your natural gifts and understanding your weaknesses. The most successful people have looked at themselves, scars and all, and are clear about who they are. If you look at great world leaders and people who have positively affected the lives of millions – Winston Churchill, Margaret Thatcher, Mother Theresa, to name a few – they understood themselves so well that they never hesitated in their actions. They were real; they were confident, and they believed in the power of their own convictions.

The most successful people also don't live their lives according to the rules. They're confident enough in their gifts to do it their way. As an entrepreneur, it's especially important to understand that if everyone did everything exactly according to the rules, it would be very hard for new things to come about. The entrepreneurs who started eBay, Google and YouTube certainly weren't thinking the way they were originally programmed to. These companies wouldn't exist if their founders hadn't chosen to color outside the lines.

When I first started my own business, I often questioned how the "experts" said things should be done. I wouldn't have been this bold if it weren't for the feelings of not fitting in that I experienced when growing up. These feelings made me not only challenge the ideas of the status quo, but also discover what was important to me. One of the main tenets of my business philosophy became: Forget what you have been told and determine for yourself if it's right for you.

I can remember when I first started to do things my way; I couldn't wait to tell my clients and have them implement the same things in their businesses. But, most of the time this fantastic new implementation failed for my clients. This really perplexed me. How could something that worked so well for me not work for everyone else? My own business coaches helped me understand why it's all about what's right for each one of us.

My first coach was someone that had been schooled extensively in understanding human behavior. This relationship helped me understand what motivates people and why they behave the way they do. This again was an uncovering of my authentic self. As I learned about other people, I learned more about myself.

My next business coach helped me understand more about fear. I learned what's really behind the feeling of fear. I discovered that fear causes a chain reaction of excuses and inaction, which in turn prevents me from reaching my vision.

Developing a more spiritual perspective is an important thing that I learned from my current business coach. Now I can look beyond a person's behavior and see the spirit within them. I can see how that spirit is trying to help the person find his or her authentic self. Different coaches have helped me at different times, depending upon what I needed to learn and where my vision was at that time.

One of my favorite movies, *Regarding Henry*, starring Harrison

Ford and Annette Bening, beautifully illustrates a man's growing awareness of his authentic self, and how that changed his vision, both of himself and his profession. Ford plays Henry, a successful New York lawyer who works for a large, prestigious firm and makes a lot of money which, of course, he uses to buy a luxurious home and fancy cars. He has made it according to the Borg. He's not a very nice person, however. By performing nasty tricks like withholding evidence in the courtroom, Henry cheats people out of money they're entitled to. He does whatever it takes to win. He also cheats on his wife and treats people badly.

While making a purchase at a corner store one evening, the place is robbed and Henry gets shot in the head. He loses some of his mental capabilities as a consequence. He can't remember his past, and doesn't have the cunning, logical mind he had before; thus, he can't practice law in the same capacity he once did. In fact, at first he can hardly speak. The people he knew before now see him as an imbecile and no longer want anything to do with him. Henry's whole world changes; but, it changes for the better. He becomes more and more in tune with his authentic self, his spiritual self. He becomes a person that you can't help but like because he is kind and considerate to everyone. He reconnects with his wife and daughter. He leaves the law firm and they live happily ever after. It's a great movie.

It shows how, by looking inward and discovering your authentic self, your passions and vision can change.

At one point in the movie, Henry is really having a hard time understanding who he is and how he fits in. (Bet you can't tell why I relate to this movie.) His physical therapist visits him and challenges Henry to ask him if he minds having bad knees. The therapist then proceeds to tell Henry the story of when his own life underwent a drastic upheaval. The therapist played football in high school, and during the championship game he went up to catch a long pass. He knew he was going to catch it and did. But as soon as he did, the defensive player on the other team tackled him and hit him in his knees. He knew when he heard his knees crack, it was all over. The football career he had trained, practiced and lived for his whole life was gone in that instant. His world changed, too, and at first, he was devastated. But during his rehabilitation, he grew to admire his physical therapist and decided that that was what he wanted to do with his life now. He could relate to people going through what he had to go through – and met people like Henry. "So, no, I don't mind having bad knees," he said to Henry. "I would have never met you otherwise." He then told Henry, "You'll figure it out just like I did."

This inspired Henry to start doing things that felt good to him and to discover his authentic self. In essence, Henry was being coached; his friend wasn't telling him what to do or how to do it, just as a coach would approach the problem. A coach doesn't have the answer for you; only you do.

This is what I strive to do for you. I give you steps to take just like Henry's physical therapist did for him. But, they're only steps. It's up to you to infuse your journey with your authenticity – and that starts with your awareness, passion and vision.

Vision

The first step to becoming a successful business owner is to have a *vision*. Most of us have an idea of what the word *vision* means, but what most of us don't realize is that vision is much more than what is typically expected as part of a formal business plan. Believe me; I didn't become successful simply because I wrote a business plan for my company. On the contrary, I do not put much credence in business plans, and do not recommend that most of my clients prepare them. My definition of vision is quite different.

Becoming an entrepreneur is ideally about moving towards something – your vision – but most of the time people go into business for themselves because they are trying to get away from something. I started my bookkeeping business because I wanted to get away from the accounting industry and thought that bookkeeping would give me the time to explore other pursuits. The problem with starting a business to get away from something is that the further you get away from it, the less excitement you have to go forward. In contrast, the more you move toward something you really want, the more excited you become.

Some of you are probably thinking that you have a vision – something to go toward that excites and motivates you. But let me ask you this: What is behind that vision? Most business people would describe their vision as a combination of revenues generated in a certain time frame, additional locations or storefronts, more employees and other objective and measurable goals, but these aren't really what a successful business person is ultimately reaching for. They don't constitute a vision. Goals are measurable things in our businesses, but why are they important to us? The answer to this question is what's really behind your vision as well as your goals. As we peel away the onion layers, keep asking yourself why these things are important to you. Let me give you a hint: It's not about the money. For many of you, your initial response to this is probably, "What?! Of course it's about the money." But, believe it or not, it's never about the money. There is a reason you want to make the money. That reason is part of your vision.

Having the *awareness* to know that it's time for personal growth – which will quickly translate to growth as a business owner – is the impetus for developing a vision that goes deeper, that comes from your authentic self. Without this awareness, your business won't move much further forward. This awareness will get you on the road to understanding what your passions are and how to connect these to your vision.

Imagine that your business is made up of a picture and a picture frame. The picture frame is the thing that supports the picture. The picture frame is made up of your goals, systems and processes, sales and marketing plans, and so forth. Most entrepreneurs spend their time working on the picture frame. Most business books and seminars focus on the picture frame. If you just get these systems in place, you'll be successful, they say. Well, what good is a picture frame with no picture? The picture is your vision. It's what you ultimately want to create. And, it's much more than that. It's not only the amount of revenue, number of storefronts and employees, and so forth, but it's also what you, the business owner, will be doing in that picture.

If it's not about the money, then how do we figure out what's behind it? How do we find the picture of what we ultimately want to be doing? I started this book by telling you the story

picture

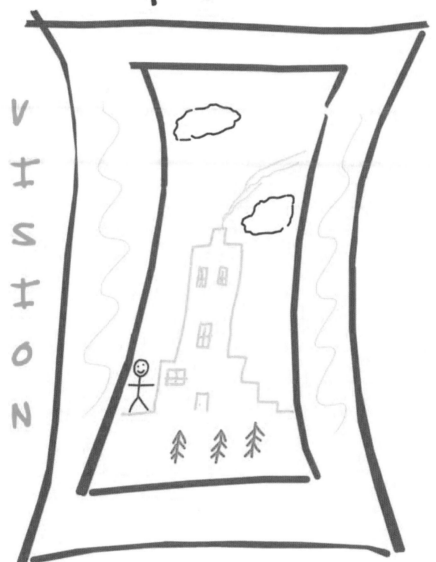

VISION

of my life. The reason I did this is because when we examine our lives, clues will surface that help us uncover our true *passions*. Before you were told what to do, when to do it and how, you did certain things without anyone telling you to. But once we start to be assimilated into society, those authentic behaviors and passions get lost. Early on, our families typically begin giving us instruction on what is acceptable behavior, morals, language, etc. This continues when we go to school. The society we live in, the friends we make, our business colleagues, our church and every part of our lives dictates to us a right way and a wrong way to do things. We're told how to dress; we even have books that tell us how to "dress for success." By the time we're adults, we've been assimilated into the Borg.

Remember when I talked about my third grade report card – the one on which I received a "C" in conduct. The Borg told me that I was doing something wrong by "helping others." No one told me to help others; I was doing this on my own. It was a natural behavior for me. Today, the passion behind my vision is how I love to help others. But when I was eight years old, I was told not to do this. Try asking yourself questions like, *when I was a child and left to my own devices, I would...* For me, this was helping others. Or, ask yourself, *when I was a child, the thing that I did the most easily was...* For me, it was using my imagination. Using our imaginations is something we are discouraged from doing early in the assimilation process, but I can't tell you how critical using my imagination has been for me in creating my vision. How about this: *When I was a child, the thing that most fascinated me was...* For me, it was learning. I continue to be fascinated by learning, not only learning more skills I can use to help others, but also learning more about myself. What parts of you have been lost through the assimilation?

This is why I wrote my life story and encourage you to do so also. Your story holds clues to your authentic self. Your authentic self is what you discover when all the onion layers are peeled away. Maybe you also remember that when I was very young I was an extrovert. I was Moon Man, and very comfortable with having an out-of-this-world sense of humor. Today, my dry, English sense of humor plays an integral role in my companies. My stepfather and the school systems discouraged this. The more I became assimilated into the Borg, the more introverted I became – to the point that I became an accountant. You can't be much more introverted than being an accountant.

Our assimilation into the box distracts us and leads us away from what we are destined to become. It's almost like before we came into this life, we said to ourselves, *let me put as many obstacles in front of me as I can to try and stop from being my authentic self, just to see if I can find myself through the maze.* The good news is that even though we get pointed in the wrong direction, it's really not the wrong direction.

When I began to look back at my life, at first it didn't seem to have any continuity; it seemed like a hodge-podge disaster. Why had I worked in so many jobs? I had not taken the path to success that most people would have taken. I didn't go to work for a large CPA firm, and then go into large industry with hopes of becoming a CFO or CEO. Instead, I went to work for small companies, and in most of them I had baptism-by-fire positions...Here, Nigel, you don't have enough time or resources to get the job done, but good luck! By most accounts I had done everything wrong, at least according to those who supposedly knew the path to success. But if I had not gone through the experience at the community college of having to learn how to be efficient under adverse circumstances, if I had not learned about systems through my

Awareness

Passion

auditing experience, if I had not started my own bookkeeping company in which I discovered there was much more to being a successful entrepreneur than financial statements, I would not have the experience, knowledge and skills to be able to help other entrepreneurs become successful. If I had gone down the Borg path to success, I would be of no use to entrepreneurial business owners. So, everything I have done has had a purpose. The experiences were a continuous evolution of learning for me to be able to help others.

The first step in creating your vision is looking from the inside out. Again, most people create a vision by creating a series of goals that their progress is measured by. These are things outside of you. Most people try to create their happiness from the outside in. They believe that as soon as they reach certain goals, magically they will be happy. Remember when I was in college trying to decide on my major? Instead of thinking about who I wanted to be in the world – who Nigel was and what was important to me – I was trying to define myself by achieving external things like the Porsche that many architects drive. I was thinking that as soon as I became an architect and made enough money to own such a car, I would be happy. This is how most of the world operates. For a time, I did too. I can remember saying to myself, *as soon as I graduate from college, I'll be happy.* Then, when I'd graduated, I would say, *as soon as I get a job, I'll be happy.* Then it was, *as soon as I pass the CPA exam, I'll be happy.* It went on and on. I realized that if I continued with this mentality, I was never going to be happy. But most people live their lives this way: Their happiness is always in the future and dictated by something outside of them. Meanwhile, in the present they are miserable. Think about what you base your happiness on. Is it something outside of you, or the passion within?

Think about this. If you won 20 million dollars in the lottery, how would your life change? Just think about that for a minute; close your eyes and think about the prospect of winning 20 million dollars. Would you continue to do the same work you are doing now? If your answer is no, then you probably aren't working with a vision that comes from your authentic self. Instead, you're probably working on accumulating things outside of you. When I ask this question, a lot of people say to me, "I would stop what I'm doing and travel around the world." But after you did all the traveling you wanted to – for a year, maybe two – then what would you do? Most people would need to do something, and most of the time it boils down to something they are passionate about. The point is that when I ask people to imagine they have won 20 million dollars – even if it's just for a moment – all the baggage they have accumulated throughout their lives as result of doing what they "should" do is suddenly gone. For a moment, the slate is clean. There is no "I should do this." There are no responsibilities; there is no right way or wrong way to do things. For a moment they are free from the Borg.

Every decision we make is unconsciously filtered through the baggage we collect over the course of our lives. And, we're not aware of this baggage most of the time. I didn't remember getting a "C" in conduct and getting in trouble for helping others until my mother sent me my third grade report card several years ago. After I received the report card, I realized how much of my behavior was dictated by this incident that happened so long ago; it was still shaping my decisions 40 years later. How many of these incidents are there? How many have I forgotten that still play a part in my life today?

Looking back at your life and the things you've done will help you uncover some of the baggage you have accumulated. It may take a lifetime to find it all. That doesn't matter. What matters is to be aware that it's there, and that you might not always be coming from your authentic self because of it. It's important to be aware of when your baggage stops you from being all you can be. The problem with being burdened by all this baggage is that it takes away your power. You stop thinking that you can create all you can because you're not free to be who you really are: your authentic self.

If you don't believe me, then consider the second part of my question regarding winning the lottery: If you would do the same thing that you were doing before you had all this money, would you do it the same way? For most people, the thought of having 20 million dollars takes away any restrictions they have placed on themselves about what they can create and how they would create it. My question to you is why aren't you doing it that way now? Most of you would say because of the money. Remember, it's not about the money. You would be surprised at what changes you can painlessly implement in your business in the next six months. Every client I've had has changed his or her vision after working with me for a little while. Most of the time their vision gets bigger and more grand, or even changes completely. Why... because they suddenly have more money? No, because I help them become aware of their baggage, and they start to eliminate its hold on them. Most of the time people only fantasize about what they can do without these restrictions, and then tell themselves, *I can't do that; let's get back to reality.* Why not? What's stopping you? It's all the baggage.

Let's recap. The reason you have a vision is that you are passionate about something. What you're passionate about is what you would do if you had no self-imposed restrictions telling you that you can't be your authentic self and that you must assimilate. And here's another hint: Passions that are connected to your authenticity are ultimately about helping people in some way, shape or form. So, how do you uncover your authentic self besides looking at what you did as a child? Remember when I told you about the partnership I was in, and that after two-plus years I was miserable? I came to realize that I was miserable not because I was going through a mid-life crisis, but because of what I was doing on a day-to-day basis.

I discovered this while attending a continuing education class entitled "The Future of the CPA Profession." Basically the instructor said, "There is no future in the CPA profession unless you become proactive at working with your clients to help them reach their goals." The more the instructor explained this, the more most of the CPAs in the class became depressed. They didn't want to go outside the box. They wanted to continue to prepare financial statements, give them to their clients and tell them, "If you have any questions, give me a call." The more the instructor spoke, the more excited I became. I was doing a little bit of this kind of work, and it felt great when I did it. I felt like I had an impact on my clients' businesses and on their success. Most of my time was spent doing tax returns, and when I thought about it, this did not excite me. In fact, the prospect of spending the rest of my life inputting tax returns and preparing financial statements in front of a computer all day depressed me. So, I began to pursue the work that felt good to me.

This is the part that most people forget about when creating their vision. What am I going to be doing on a day-to-day, hour-to-hour, minute-to-minute basis when I reach my ultimate vision? I know a lot of business owners that put a practical vision together with incredible details about the revenues they want to generate and how they're going to generate them, but they don't think about what they'll actually be doing all day, every day. When they reach their vision, they hate what they're doing and are miserable. Start thinking about what you want to do when you get to your vision, and then start putting the plans together to make that happen now.

I told my partners in the CPA firm of my vision, but they could not see it as I did. Eventually, our visions were so far apart that I was asked to leave the partnership. After reflecting for several months, I got excited again because I thought I could now pursue my passion without my former partners stopping me. The point of this is that the authentic self simply likes to do things that it likes. You certainly don't tell yourself, *I'm going to do all these things this weekend that I hate to do.* But we do this in business because of our assimilation. To know if you are going in the direction toward your authentic self, ask yourself, *does this feel good; does it feel right?* The more I pursued helping others proactively with their businesses, the more it felt good and right. So, is your vision really what you would do if you could? Does what you'd be doing feel right on a day-to-day, hour-to-hour, minute-to-minute basis?

Many entrepreneurs get to this point and find that while they can answer these questions honestly, they don't know how to act upon their answers. The idea of expanding your vision or creating a completely new one probably seems incredibly overwhelming. You might even think that your vision is simply unrealistic and out of reach – that it would take a lifetime to get there, and you don't have time for that. But I'm here to tell you that the opposite is true – that you can make things happen for yourself and your business right now. You can get remarkably closer to your vision by just planning on changing one thing in the next six months that would make it more fun for you to be at work. And often I can help you make this change happen in half that time or even less. It starts with moving you out of the comfort zone that you're currently residing in. Which brings us to the next step...

Comfort Zones

A *comfort zone* is when you stop at a certain place for a length of time and don't go forward. The comfort zone may not even necessarily be comfortable, but you know what to expect there. You might have a sales cycle that goes up and down and creates cash flow problems. But because you have experienced it for a length of time, you know what to expect and how to deal with it, financially and emotionally. You got to where you are in life and business by going through a series of comfort zones, and you'll reach your vision by going through another series of them. Imagine that your comfort zones are a series of picture frames that connect where you are now to your ultimate vision. The frames will become stronger as you progress forward to your vision. The pictures within the frames will also become clearer.

As I've mentioned in the last chapter, once you create your vision, most of you will find the distance between where you are and where you want to go quite overwhelming. When you start to think about what you have to do, you get stuck in a maze. The overwhelming feeling keeps you in the comfort zone even longer. So instead of thinking of all the things you have to do in order to reach your vision, think about what you would like to change in the next six months. As you think about this, remember that we're connecting to your vision, and that your authentic self wants to do things that are fun and energizing.

To get things started, I want you to think about the tasks that you do each day. If your business is a one-person show, you'll obviously have a lot to think about because you do everything in the business. I call these business owners *Egopre-*

neurs because it's all about them; "It's my business" is the prevailing mindset at this stage. Hopefully you started your business by going after something you're passionate about. But whether you did or not, if you're an Egopreneur, you'll end up performing tasks that you're good at, bad at and love to do. You might have started the business with the intention of doing the things you love to do, but because you're doing everything, you necessarily end up doing tasks that you're good at (but don't like) and bad at as well.

No one is good at everything. It doesn't take a rocket scientist to know that when we do tasks we are bad at, we won't do a very good job. Again, we don't say we're going to do things we dislike on the weekends, so why do we do it in business? I know what you're saying... because we have to; we have no choice; we can't afford not to. First you have to become aware of the tasks you are bad at, even if you think you can't get out of doing these tasks. Then look at how well you are doing these tasks. You probably don't like doing them because you don't do them well, and thus relegate them to the back burner where they usually boil over and make a big mess. Having worked as an accountant for the past 30 years, I know that most people are not good at the task of bookkeeping and accounting. But software programs like QuickBooks have convinced most small business owners that they can do the bookkeeping and accounting functions themselves. Regardless of what you do to try to make this task more palatable for yourself, if you don't like doing it, you will probably create incorrect and inaccurate financial information, and it will likely not be up to date, yielding negative results for your business.

So, make a list of things you are bad at, good at, and love to do. The tasks you are bad at should be easy to determine. Just ask yourself, *what do I hate to do?* Determining which tasks we're good at compared to the tasks we love to do can

be more complicated. Many times we get these two mixed up. How do we tell the difference, and why is this difference important? It took me a long time to figure this out. Shouldn't we do the tasks we're good at? Let me answer this way: After I have done 10 hours of preparing tax returns – which I am good at doing – I'm not ready to go out and party, believe me. However, after doing 10 hours of business coaching, I'm ready for anything. The difference is that the tasks we are simply good at drain us; the tasks we love to do rejuvenate us. It's important to be aware of the distinction. Again, going back to when I was in my CPA partnership and I was preparing more complicated tax returns... my ego enjoyed the fact that I could do them, but the more I did them, the more drained I became.

Eventually the Egopreneur hits a ceiling just as I did after starting my own business. There are only so many hours in the day, and after you reach a certain volume of business, you can't handle any more. To remedy this, many Egopreneurs work like crazy for several years. They typically work many hours a day, seven days a week, thinking that they'll hit a volume of revenue that allows them to hire someone to help. The problem is, how long will that take? In the meantime, how does that affect your ability to be competitive, to operate effectively, and how much does that drain you physically, mentally and emotionally?

Once Egopreneurs hit this ceiling, they have a couple of choices. Of course, they can continue doing what they've been doing. Eventually this will take its toll. They can reduce the volume, or go out of business. Or, they can evolve to the *Entrepreneur*.

The Entrepreneur is the business owner that has gone beyond the ceiling of the Egopreneur, and has either outsourced some tasks, delegated them, or both. The company has grown beyond just the business owner. This can be a challenging, rewarding and frustrating next step. Indeed, many Egopreneurs never evolve to the Entrepreneur, and many Entrepreneurs never make it. Why is this next step so hard, and why do so many business owners fail? The reasons are numerous. If you talk to financial experts, they might say that the business owner didn't have enough capital invested. If you talk to consultants, they' probably say the business owner didn't have adequate systems. If you talk to management people, they might say that the business owner didn't have anyone managing the company. And, my favorite: If you talk to your mother, she might say you were never good at this, so why did you think you'd be successful in the first place? The point is that everyone has their opinion depending on where they are coming from.

But what's really happening to business owners as they move from Egopreneurs to Entrepreneurs? When it comes to how they approach business, people can be categorized in one of three ways: the technician, the manager and the leader. The technician is the person that does the work in the business. To this person time is money. If he or she can't see it or touch it, it doesn't exist. Remember my stepfather? As a mechanic, he was a technician. He worked with his hands... he could touch it. The manager is the person in the business that manages systems, which might include managing people. To this person, time is profit. The manager wants to know how to make more money by making the systems more efficient. The leader is the person in the company that comes up with new ideas; he or she looks at the big picture and creates something bigger than just him or her. To the leader, time is value. This person wants to know how to continually make the company more valuable. Who do you think starts most entrepreneurial businesses? It's the technician. This person works in a very small comfort

Product Development

Marketing

Sales

EGO-preneur

Admin

Product Delivery

Accounting

zone and does all the work. The technicians that start small businesses do so because they're trying to get away from something: bosses they don't like, or simply having someone try to control them. They might have been able to be technically proficient at their skills before they started their own businesses. This doesn't necessarily make them good business owners, though. Usually they're not. They have a limited vision, work by themselves and don't understand or appreciate the value of management and leaders. Because they are experts who do all the work, they're usually more successful at the Egopreneur level than they are at the Entrepreneur level. Once they evolve to the Entrepreneur level, they seldom change from being the expert. This causes them to have limited growth potential because they end up doing what they wanted to get away from in the first place: controlling everything.

The number one reason that small business owners fail is because they don't evolve beyond being experts. The transition from expert to professional business owner is very difficult because regardless of which approach the business owner has – technician, manager or leader – none of them alone has all the skills required to be a professional business owner. But if entrepreneurial business owners do not make that transition, they're rarely successful. The professional business owner has to understand and appreciate the skills of all three – technician, manager and leader. This can be a tall order, because in essence, when the Egopreneur tries to transform into the professional business owner/CEO, the dynamic can conflict with what the business owner's authentic self wants. These two dynamics – the emergence of the business owner's authentic self and the need to become CEO – need to happen simultaneously.

In order for business owners to be happy, they have to

bring out their authentic selves. They must also look at all the pieces of the puzzle and make sure each one is in place. I remember how this dynamic played out when I started consulting with my clients very early on about setting up their systems. I had helped one of my clients set up all the needed systems, hire and train the right people for the right positions, create marketing and sales plans and so forth. Everything was in place for the company to be really successful. But the business owner had not made the transition to being the CEO of the company, and all he cared about was developing new products. Even though everything was in place, no one was running the company. Eventually, everything collapsed. At the time I couldn't understand what had happened. I now know that the business owner's conflict between being the CEO and being his authentic self had not been resolved.

I'm not insisting that you have to become the CEO of your business and remain in that position. But if you go beyond the Egopreneur, this dynamic will occur, and it will have a great affect on the business. Ultimately, you want to create a business where you as the owner will be doing only the tasks that you love to do. In order to get there, you will have to become the CEO for awhile. This means you have to understand everything in the business; you have to know the importance of how each piece of the puzzle fits in place to create the picture you want. You can't just say one day when you discover what you love to do, okay, *that's all I'm going to do from now on.* Only wanting to do the things they love to do and not dealing with all the other aspects of the business is the reason why so many would-be entrepreneurs start businesses only to soon abandon them and go to work for someone else. They decide they don't want to deal with marketing and sales, billing or product development... or whatever tasks they don't love doing. This is the difference between the entrepreneur and the

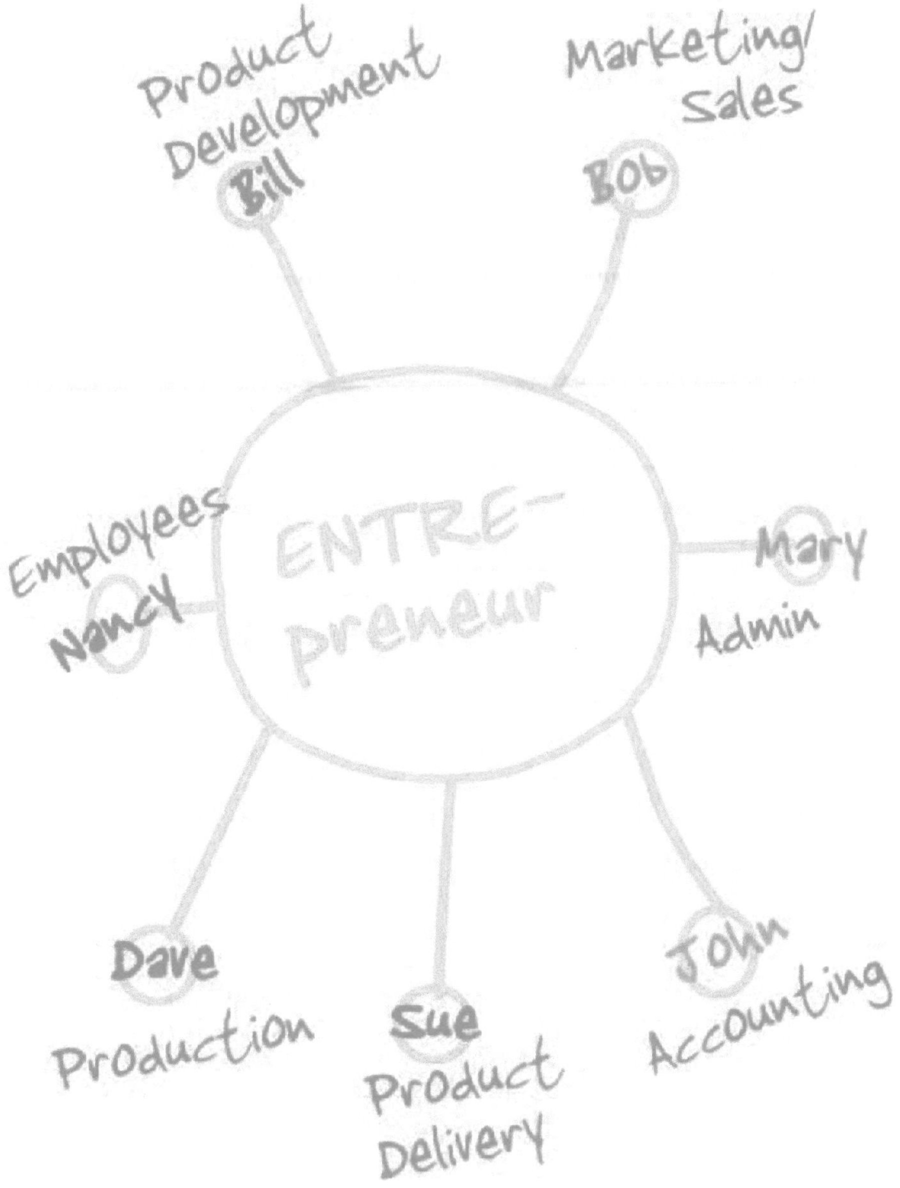
Product Development
Bill
Marketing/ Sales
Bob
Employees
Nancy
ENTRE-preneur
Mary
Admin
Dave
Production
Sue
Product Delivery
John
Accounting

employee. No matter how much the entrepreneur doesn't like to perform certain tasks or be responsible for certain things, the thought of working for someone else is much worse.

The reason this transition from Egopreneur to Entrepreneur is so difficult for most business owners is twofold. First, by the time the transition occurs, business owners are exhausted from doing everything as the Egopreneur. When they started their businesses, all they were thinking about having to do was sell their products or services. Then they discovered they had to do all these other tasks in the business. Even though this is frustrating to them, the fact that revenues are going up and the client base is growing keeps feeding their egos. But by the time they are forced to transition by having to hire employees or outsource, they are exhausted. They have been doing everything for a long time and working very hard. Consequently, not much thought is put into how this transition is going to take place. It becomes simply a matter of the business owner wanting someone to take things off his or her hands. Because this transition is not very well thought out, systems are usually not in place. After all, the business owner didn't need systems before because there was only one person in the business then. If there are any systems at all, they reside mostly in the business owner's head. Eventually, this lack of planning creates chaos in the company. As time goes by, the business owner realizes that the person he or she hired isn't handling tasks with the same sense of urgency and quality as the business owner would. The results can be detrimental to the business.

The second reason the transition from Egopreneur to Entrepreneur is so hard, is that business owners, having to become more involved in all the pieces of the puzzle, often feel like they're going in the wrong direction. When they start to implement systems in order to clone themselves, they're officially not having fun anymore. They could tolerate these problems when they were still operating solo, but now they have to bring their plans out of their heads and onto paper. They start pleading with themselves, *wasn't the whole idea for me to find my passion and only do the things I love to do? Now I'm doing all these things I hate to do. This can't be right...I must be doing something wrong.* This confusion is further amplified by the feeling that doing the things they hate to do will go on indefinitely.

This is why I help my clients become *Ultrapreneurs*. The problem with both the Egopreneur and the Entrepreneur is they are both trapped in their businesses. Even if Entrepreneurs make it through the transition and have systems in place, they are usually still involved in everything in the business. The Entrepreneurs are still the ones making all the decisions, just as when they were Egopreneurs, and nothing gets done without them being in the middle of it. So, what they have created for themselves is a bigger and better trap than they had before. They're rarely able to take vacations or get away from the business for any period of time.

The Ultrapreneur is the business owner that has transitioned beyond Entrepreneur. They're the business owners that only do the things they love in the business and have systems in place to make sure all the other pieces of the puzzle are in place. Ultrapreneurs have resolved the two dynamics of the successful business owner: the passion of the authentic self and the need to be the CEO of the business.

The fact is, as an Entrepreneur you will have to spend more time on things you don't like to do, but it won't be forever. But the more time you spend on understanding and appreciating how all the pieces fit together and creating systems that work for you, the less time you will eventually have to spend doing things you don't like. If you don't spend some time working on

ULTRA-preneur

Product
Development

Marketing/
Sales

Bill

Bob

Employees

Nancy

Admin

Mary

Dave

Sue

John

Production

Product
Delivery

Accounting

your systems, the weaknesses there will keep coming back to haunt you, and you will end up spending a lot of time working on things you don't like to do. I know what your question is at this point: How do we know what to start on first? When you look at all the tasks that have to be accomplished, it's overwhelming.

Again, we'll look at just the next six months, and perhaps surprisingly for you, we'll start with your worst fear. The comfort zone that you're in is defined by the perceived obstacle that's preventing you from moving past the comfort zone. When I tell you that we can overcome your biggest obstacle – and thus move through a comfort zone – much sooner than six months, you might be excited at first, but you'll quickly realize your fears surrounding this accelerated time frame. Your vision is suddenly right in front of your face, but I want you to look it in the eye. For most people, fear stems from the thought of losing something... *I don't know how to handle these changes in this short amount of time, so I'm probably going to fail and lose my business in the process.* This is the right side of your brain – your imagination – which is otherwise a good thing, running wild. When this happens, I help you to access your left side – your rational side – by asking you to find evidence to support your fear. My clients never come up with any solid evidence.

Fear can be a great business tool because it tells you what you need to work on the most. The wonderful thing about fears is that they naturally come up in priority order. In other words, your biggest fear comes up first, and this is what you should start working on now because it is the main thing that's keeping you from going forward. Fear doesn't go away until you solve the thing that's causing it. And fear gives you a heads up; it is present long before what you are afraid of becomes a reality. Best of all, the more you face your fears and move through your comfort zones, the more comfortable this process gets.

I know that most of you are asking, *how can I do this when I don't have time to do what I'm doing now? How can I do even more? I'm overwhelmed, frustrated and exhausted.*

Let's look at simple ways to utilize your time...

Time

Time is one thing we cannot buy. Of course, we can work our fingers to the bone by putting in as many hours as it takes, seven days a week if necessary, but sooner or later, this will cause us and our businesses to unravel. Yet, many Egopreneurs and Entrepreneurs do just this, convincing themselves that *I'll just keep working harder and eventually everything will work out.* Unfortunately, it won't, and eventually you'll start to lose your health, your family and yourself.

I'll admit that I used to entertain myself with a lovely daydream involving a wizard who stealthily approached my bassinette while I lay fresh and newborn in the hospital maternity wing, tapped my forehead with his gnarled, wizardy finger and muttered a spell that magically gave me more hours in my days than the average schmoes who only got 24. Though I was keenly aware of the fantastical nature of my daydream, when I first ran my own business, I'd often work as if I really did have more than 24 hours between days; and I've already explained the resulting frustration. Everyone has the same amount of time as everyone else. So why do some business owners become successful and others don't? Some of you are probably thinking this is because they have more money. I have known plenty of people that have money that didn't become successful. You probably do too. But, you argue, it sure helps. This might be true, but if you don't spend your time wisely, you can still lose your business even with a lot of money. Think about how many businesses borrow the money they think they need to become successful and yet fail. Money is no guarantee for success.

The first shift in thinking that has to occur is for you to look at how you're spending your time. When looking at the next comfort zone, begin looking at it through the eyes of the two dynamics, the authentic self and the CEO. I'll repeat a question I've asked you earlier: What things would you like to change in the next six months that would make things more fun for you? The long term goals will come from what the authentic self wants. The short term goals will come from the needs of the CEO. The two must be in line with each other. If you don't have a vision of where you are ultimately going, how do you know you are making the right decisions in the present and short term? That's like having the Thelma and Louise business plan. Remember the end of the movie, when they accelerated their car and went off the cliff? You might be able to accelerate your business without having a vision, but it will eventually go right off the cliff.

Remember that the ultimate goal is for you to be doing only those things you love to do. Start by looking at the things you don't want to do. In order to stop doing those things, first look at how efficiently and effectively you are doing these things. How can you do them better and faster? The better and faster you can do these tasks, the less time you have to spend doing them.

But, I don't have the time, you say. Sure you do. Even though you are very busy and work incredible hours, how much of that time is spent working toward your vision? Most of the time, business owners spend their time being distracted from working toward their vision. Why? Because most of the time business owners have only developed the necessity part of their vision. This part includes revenues, multiple locations, employees and so forth. They have no idea why they want to create these things, except for the notion that it's about the money. They have no longing to get to the point where

TASKS

- bad
- good
- love

they're working only on things they love to do. Instead, it's about doing a bunch of things they hate to do for an extended length of time, and the payoff is that they get to stop doing it at some point in the future when they're able to retire. While they might have the incentive to get there as fast as possible, what happens when things don't go according to plan? What happens when things take longer than expected? Of course, I've never seen a business that doesn't go according to plan...my dry English humor is at work again. Things rarely go according to plan, and when they don't, business owners get frustrated. What keeps them going when they don't have the passion part of their vision in place? Not much, because the fact that those things are going to take longer than expected means the business owners will have to spend more time doing the things they don't like and even hate to do.

But how would it be different if you knew what the passion part of your vision was? If you knew that no matter how much money you won from the lottery, you'd still be doing the same thing... How would that change the way you looked at speed bumps and potholes along the way? And also knowing that doing some of the things that you don't really like to do in order to take on the role of CEO would take as long or short as you put your mind to it... How would that change your attitude when things didn't go according to plan? Think about it...You will eventually be able to do what you love, and it will happen in a surprisingly limited amount of time. Business owners spend most of their time being distracted because they don't have the passion part of their vision in place, and for them, getting to the ultimate vision seems too far away.

I know that many of you are still thinking that you really don't have the time, so let's look for a moment at the logical shift that needs to be made regarding time. What would happen if today someone in your family got hurt or was sick enough to be taken to the hospital? Would you continue working because you didn't have time for that? Of course not. As soon as you found out, you'd rush to the hospital. What would happen if you stayed there all day as well as the next day? Would your business go under? If it did, you were on very thin ice to begin with. But most business owners would not be put out of business by taking that amount of time away from their working days. If might cause some difficulties and backups, but they could recover fairly easily.

Now think about taking 30 minutes a day and using that time to work on things you need to change in the next six months. Okay, let's take just 15 minutes a day – the amount of time for a coffee break. If you take 15 minutes a day to work on your six-month goals, this would translate into one hour and 15 minutes a week. In two weeks, this would add up to two and a half hours, and in a month, five hours. In six months, this would mean 30 hours. What results could you achieve if you worked on something for 30 hours? That's almost like taking a week off in a six month period. But you can't do this because you don't have the time...right? While you might not be able to take a week off to work on your vision, I'll bet that you can afford to spend 15 minutes a day on it. In a year, you could spend 60 hours working on reaching your vision. And if you did use 30 minutes a day instead of 15, this would add up to 120 hours in a year – almost three weeks. Think about what you could accomplish if you took three weeks off each year to work on reaching your vision. The more time you can squeeze out of your day, the faster you will reach your vision. Again, this is possible because you know what the passion part of your vision is, and you now know that you can accelerate getting to your vision.

Once you make strides toward your vision, you can begin

putting systems in place to make sure things run as they should when you get to that place where you do only the things you love.

Systems

To most entrepreneurial business owners, *systems* should be a four-letter word. True entrepreneurs are very creative. They like to work on the big picture vision. To them, systems are mundane and simply boring – even something they hate to do. Thus, they're usually terrible at implementing them. But systems are necessary for business owners to become Ultrapreneurs.

You're probably thinking that you knew there was going to be a catch to all of this. First I start off by telling you to find your true passion and the things you love to do, and now I involve you in systems. I've got some nerve. Well, here's the difference: Most systems, like everything else in business are usually created from the outside in. Remember when I talked about vision and how most business owners create the necessity part of the vision without knowing why they are creating it? This is a prime example of creating from the outside in. The entrepreneur thinks, *as soon as I create all of these things outside of myself, then magically I'll know why I created it, and magically, I'll be happy.* Wrong. It's the same way with creating systems; they have to be created from the inside out. In essence when you transition from the small Egopreneur to the larger Entrepreneur, you're creating things by expanding yourself. And though this step is all about you, it's not the same thing that's going on with Egopreneurs. The difference is that you create systems not to give your ego more attention, but to bring you closer to your vision. It's all about bringing it from inside yourself – your authentic self – out into your business. That's what you're doing when you pull out the systems you have in your head and put them on paper. You are manifesting yourself in your business.

Maybe this will help to illustrate the idea: Have you ever known a really disorganized business owner that has a very organized business? Usually if the business owner is disorganized, so is the business. Whatever is going on with the business owner will usually manifest itself in the business. So if the business owner doesn't take any time or have any appreciation for systems, the business will have inadequate systems.

As with everything else in a successful business, the process of creating systems starts with looking at yourself. I want you to ask yourself what things keep coming up over and over again that distract you from working on your vision. These things keep coming up because you don't have adequate systems in place. Until you put them in place, they will keep taking you away from working on your vision. For example, when I first started my bookkeeping and accounting business I used to answer the telephone every time it rang. I was so afraid that if I didn't I might miss an important call and lose a client. At first this was no problem. But as I grew, and especially during tax season, this became a big problem. When tax season was in full swing, the phone would literally ring all day long. The question most people had when they called was, "When are my tax returns going to be finished?" If I answered the phone all day long, I certainly wasn't able to work on anyone's taxes. This caused me to work into the night and be extremely exhausted by the end of tax season. I had no system in place to take care of this problem, but the problem began with me, not my clients. It was my insecurity about losing a client that ironically created a situation where I could have easily lost many clients by not completing their tax returns on time.

So, start looking for systems that you need but haven't created yet because of your skewed view of the way things should run in your business. Again, is the situation that keeps coming up over and over again fun for you? Answering the phones all day and working on tax forms all night definitely wasn't fun for me. I eventually took blocks of time where I didn't answer the phone and let the calls go to voice mail. I would check my messages later, and at designated times I would return any calls I felt I needed to. During subsequent tax seasons, I would give my clients a turnaround time for completion as soon as they brought me their tax information, which eliminated most of the calls. The point is that I had to look inside myself to see where the problem was coming from and devise a system to resolve it.

Most business owners hire someone else to create a one-size-fits-all system for them and then try to squeeze into it. There are all kinds of books and seminars that will teach you how to do everything correctly. Remember the book *Dress for Success*. And a couple of weeks ago I read an article on Yahoo that proclaimed the right things and wrong things to include in your business wardrobe this year. I wonder who these people are that try to dictate what I wear; they certainly don't know me. There are a lot of people that think they know the answer, and they think it's not only the answer for them, but for you as well. If this is true, since there are so many books on how to be rich and thin, we should all be rich and thin. And why are there so *many* books about bring rich and thin? Shouldn't there only be one? I've seen a lot of business owners go to this seminar and that seminar, read this book and that book, only to end up with a collage of many people's visions, time management techniques and so forth, but not their own. They follow a certain book for awhile and then it becomes passé, so they go for the new "in" book and follow that for awhile. This keeps going on and on, but they don't seem to move forward toward their vision and goals. They seem to think *all I have to do is find the right book and then I'll be successful,* or *if I accumulate enough knowledge by reading these books and going to all these seminars, eventually I'll find the secret to my success.*

It doesn't come from the outside in; it comes from the inside out. This is true for your vision, both the passionate part and the necessity part, and it's true for your systems as well. There is no right answer, only the answer that's right for you. So when you look at how you're spending your time and start discovering the things that keep coming up over and over again that require systems to resolve them, don't look to others to find the answer for you. It's inside you. You just have to look for it.

And remember, you are creative. Understand your strengths and how to use them. This means that you don't have to sit down and write the systems out on paper yourself if writing is not your strength. If this is your dilemma, have someone else who has this strength do it for you. It just has to come from inside you. The most important thing to keep in mind as you think about the systems that you would like to implement is that you should only do things in a way that is natural for you. Several years ago, when I was in the midst of creating a new marketing plan for my company, I was told by everyone who knew something about marketing that a blog was essential to my business. The problem was, writing simply isn't my strength and consequently I don't enjoy it. The thought of having to churn out a new page of pithy and clever observations each week sounded about as fun as filing endless stacks of tax returns. It just wasn't a natural fit for me. So I tapped my strengths – which include talking, not writing – and came up with a video style blog instead. I felt much happier about this, and I approach my blog with gusto now. If you're a natural collaborator but you try to do things solo, it won't work for

picture frame

systems

supports the picture

your business. Or, you might try to become a boss figure as you transition to Entrepreneur and hire employees, when in fact, you don't actually enjoy managing people. Just be you. You can still give direction by having systems in place that keep things organized.

Even though I can't give you the answers, I can give you a simple technique for creating systems that has worked well for me and my clients. When you are looking at creating a system, ask yourself these three questions: What information do I need to know? From whom? And, when? Not only can you use this technique to begin to create a system for yourself, but it can be used to create the systems required for all aspects of a business, including your employees. How you implement this into a system is up to you. For a lot of my clients this has become a checklist that turns into policies, that turns into job descriptions. Again, you are taking what's inside of you and manifesting it into the business. When you were the Egopreneur, you knew what information you needed, who you needed it from, and when you needed it. When you evolve to the Entrepreneur, this information has to get out so that others can use it when it's appropriate for them to do so. Once you start to do this, you will find that it's not so hard to refine any system you set up. In fact, it becomes fun. If it doesn't become fun, you're either not bringing things from the inside out, or you're not using your strengths to do so.

The more you do things in a natural way, the easier running your business becomes. You'll see more and more of your authentic self coming forward, and as this happens, you'll soon find yourself working in a way that's 100 percent authentic. It's when you reach this point that you are ready to evolve to Ultrapreneur.

The Body, Mind, and Soul of Your Business

You've learned about the three stages of business evolution – Egopreneur, Entrepreneur and Ultrapreneur – and the four steps – vision, comfort zones, time and systems – that help move you through these stages of evolution. You have also discovered how authenticity is the wonderful, crucial thread that runs through this whole process. Now we're going to discuss the five elements that make up a successful business and how all of these seemingly fragmented, confusing pieces fit together in a very simple way to form a solid base for your business to stand upon.

The first element of a successful business is, quite simply, *understanding business*. Most people who say they're going to be business owners or entrepreneurs have passion and great ideas, but they don't understand how business really works... what the pieces are, why they're important and how they interact. It's essential that every piece be given the proper attention or your business will suffer. For example, my accounting company utilizes a software program that looks at six areas of my clients' businesses: cash flow, profit, sales, employees, borrowing and assets. It tells them whether or not a certain area is getting stronger or weaker. If there is a weak area, and it's not taken care of, it can affect the other areas; it's like a cancer, and it spreads. Sometimes what seems like a weakness in one area is really coming from a weakness in another area; it's just a symptom.

I've seen many clients experience increasing sales, and say to themselves, *isn't that great*, only to soon find that their cash flow isn't so great. On paper it might look fine: sales are going up, and accounts receivable are plentiful. But, when we look at all the pieces, we discover that there's a collection problem – that the business owner is not getting those receivables for 45 to 60 days, creating a cash flow problem. Often, before he or she comes to me, the business owner has borrowed money to remedy this cash flow problem and gotten further into debt. Many business owners might try to dismiss such troubles as timing problems, but when they look at the red ink, they wonder, *am I doing the right thing?* I've seen sales go up and bottom lines go up, and people still go out of business because they cannot pay for their debt out of that bottom line.

As a business owner, you need to understand and stay on top of your accounts receivable and accounts payable, and know how to convert that into a cash flow projection. You need to know if and when you can hire an employee, and be aware of whether you're getting a return on the assets you've used to hire that person. You need to know if your cash flow will service your borrowing. What decisions are you making and how are these decisions affecting all of the other aspects of your business?

Understanding business doesn't mean that you have to learn how to read financial statements. I actually don't advocate that at all. But, as a business owner, you do need to have awareness and an understanding of these things to the point where you can honestly call yourself a businessperson. You don't have to *do* it, but you have to *understand* it.

Gaining this understanding is an educational process, and it's something that I do with my clients mostly through group coaching. In these sessions, my clients get the opportunity to interact with other business owners like themselves, and we have powerful discussions about the problems that arise in small businesses, how to understand what causes these problems and how to implement effective solutions. Once you gain this full understanding of business, you only need to spend five minutes a week reviewing the pieces to make sure everything's on track.

The next element in a successful business is *passionate creation*. We've talked some about passion in the book already, but let me reiterate here by saying that a *passionate creation* is something that really excites you and is important to you beyond just making money. Usually it has something to do with what's happened to you in your life. It's the continuation of a theme, if you will, that has recurred throughout much of your life experience. Most of the time, it involves helping others with something that you have needed help with your-self. If this connection is present, then your approach to your business is really passionate because, having gone through the same thing yourself, you naturally understand what your customers are going through.

For me, gaining all of the skills, knowledge and awareness that it takes to be a successful business owner took a long time because I didn't have a mentor or coach to help me figure it out. While there were opportunities for people in corporate America to get coaching, there weren't coaches who worked with small business owners like me. It became a passion of mine to understand the confusion, fear and all the things that small business owners go through – and to help others wade through it quickly and easily so they could implement things in their own businesses. There's a strong connection between my coaching and what I've gone through myself. If I can help somebody realize that they're passionate about something and that they can make a living out of that passion, it's really fulfilling to me – and it's fulfilling to them, of course. That's what I mean by *passionate creation*.

The third element is *authenticity*. Again, we've discussed authenticity at length already, but it is crucial to business owners because it's not possible to be really successful if you're not authentic. Even if you've got the passionate creation, without authenticity you won't have great creative capacity or power. If you're not sincere about what you're doing, and you're simply not being you, people can tell – even if they can't exactly put their finger on it. The more authentic you are, the more power you have to create what you want to create. Authenticity frees you from all those restrictions that you were taught as you grew up. For many people, being authentic is, at first, like being naked. They think, *oh my gosh, everybody can see everything about me because I'm not holding anything back.* Very quickly, however, an authentic person can feel comfortable in this state. It's like saying, *there are things I need to improve about me, but I'm working on it. This is who I am right now, and I feel good about that.* Authenticity is incredibly freeing, and it empowers you to make strong decisions and do things without worrying about how other people are going to view your actions.

Also important to a successful business is *day-to-day happiness*. There's a difference between *passionate creation* and being happy with what you're doing on a day-to-day, hour-to-hour, minute-to-minute basis. And, it's not just being happy with what you're doing, but being happy with who you are and where you are. You can be passionate about creating something, and excited to do it in your business, and yet hate what you have to do to get there. Therefore, you're miserable until you reach your goal. Living your life for future happiness is not enjoying the fullness of life. Day-to-day happiness is about enjoying the journey. It's about working in a way that is natural to you, and that is fun and exciting, so that you're enjoying *all* of it. Is there something in your day – no mattter how small or simple – that you'd like to do differently? For example, you might dislike sitting at a desk. Why

74

not do your work standing up or walking around as much as possible? If it makes you happier and doesn't harm production, there's no reason why you shouldn't make the change. Day-to-day happiness also frees you up to be more aware, and that awareness allows you to be more creative. When you have happiness on a day-to-day basis, things come faster to you. It makes everyone who works around you happy, too. They feel a stronger connection to you and are much more likely to be productive.

Knowing *your market* is the last of the five elements to a successful business. What I'm talking about here is knowing what your business is trying to carve out. What is your purpose in the market? What do you bring to the table? What is different about your business compared to your competition? This is not the same thing as stating your company's mission. Rather, *your market* is something that you constantly look at, and it could be changing on a continuous basis. Ask yourself, *what are the needs or demands that are out there, and are we fulfilling them? What piece of that do we want to fulfill?* The answer will likely be different depending upon the industry that you're serving.

Years ago, a sporting goods store – after deciding that youth athletes made up one of its target markets – discovered that one of the things that junior high, high school and college kids wanted to do in sports was to be able to jump higher. The store employed people who could show these athletes what kinds of exercises they could do to develop their leg muscles and these experts conducted in-store clinics to this end. The store also promoted products that would appeal to young athletes trying to improve their vertical leaps: the right shoes, trampolines and so forth. However, this business wasn't just selling sporting goods; it was contributing to the lives of young people and making a difference. It was a win-win situation. This was the piece that this sporting goods business carved out in the market, and it brought it back as a profit center for the business. The program was so successful that many sporting goods companies today do the same thing. The store could also do something similar with other profit centers from other markets that it identifies, such as helping retired people to be more active by helping them to get more limber. The markets will all have a common theme, though, which is to help people to perform better in sports.

My market happens to be helping entrepreneurial businesses succeed because, not only do I believe that small business is the backbone of America, but I can completely relate to what my clients are going through, since I experienced the same things. I don't have this linear formula that somebody else made up and I try to make my clients follow. As I'm working with my clients, I'm saying, *yes, I remember how that felt and all the things that went with it,* and I can help clients get through entrepreneurial struggles a lot faster than it took me to do it because I didn't have somebody mentoring me.

It's also important to know that you must continually look at your market, and that it will probably change over time. In my business, for example, I've noticed changes when it comes to virtual coaching versus face-to-face coaching. When coaching first became popular, the majority of it was done virtually, and many coaches still do it almost exclusively this way. I coach most of my clients face-to-face, and I think the current trend is moving toward more face-to-face interactions. However, I can see the benefits of both. With virtual coaching, I can expand my geographic reach – which is something I'm considering – but at the same time, speaking with clients in person is much more powerful. I'm discovering that I can mix the two methods. When gas prices go up or there's a snowstorm, and my clients don't want to drive to meet with me, we can use the virtual coaching session as a backup. As you can see, your market is an elastic concept.

Now, let's put all of the pieces that you've learned about here and throughout the book into a cohesive whole, which becomes the Body, Mind and Soul of your business. The Body includes the three stages of business evolution: the *Egopreneur,* the *Entrepreneur* and the *Ultrapreneur;* the four steps: *vision, comfort zones, time and systems;* and *understanding business.* The Body represents the tangible parts of business.

The next part is the Mind, which includes *passionate creation* and *your market.* This is where you're really thinking about what you're creating and what impact it is going to have on people. The Mind takes you beyond just selling products or services for money. The Body is like an ice cream store, while the Mind is *what flavor are we going to be?*

The Soul includes *authenticity* and complete *day-to-day happiness.* It's enjoying yourself. It's being all you can be. It's you, the business owner, not worrying about being someone you think you should be in order to be successful. When your business's Soul is intact, you are being totally yourself and still are successful. In fact, the Soul makes you more successful, because people are attracted to that sincerity.

The Body, Mind and Soul are like a three-legged stool. If one of the legs is weak and wobbly, then the stool falls over and your business is not successful. And, that's what I often see. I see many people work on the Body and Mind, but the Soul isn't really there. These business owners aren't being authentic and aren't really happy. You get the complete package only when all three of these legs are working. What this three-legged stool does is it creates the life that the business owner wants. It gives you what you want on a day-to-day basis. It's what's important to you. It helps you discover what you want to have

YOUR BUSINESS

BODY
- 3 Stages
- 4 Steps
- Understanding Business

MIND
- Passionate creation
- Your Market

SOUL
- Authentic Self
- Complete Day-to-day Happinenss

an impact on. And you create your business based on these personal things.

You'll notice that this stool is not a linear concept. It includes several things of equal importance happening simultaneously. This is what I'm keenly aware of when I'm coaching. My client might be looking at one specific thing, but that one thing could have several different dynamics working at once. The client doesn't see this at first. He or she is thinking, *as soon as I finish this, I can go on to the next thing.* I show them that there are always four or five things happening at one time, and that they must all be worked on or one of the legs might come loose and cause the whole thing to collapse.

Having these five elements in place and ensuring their strength is what finally brings you to the level of Ultrapreneur. In fact, these elements are necessary to becoming an Ultrapreneur. Doing the things that you want to do in your business – being authentic – is crucial, of course, to being successful. But the other elements that we've just discussed must also exist along with your authenticity in the Body, Mind and Soul of your business so that your business can stand strong for as long as you want it to.

So instead of saying, *I've got certain things that I want – a house, a car, money for my family – so I've got to get a business that makes money, and with that money, I can have all this stuff,* it's really *here's the life that I want, and now I'm going to build a business that will give me that life.* With the Body, Mind and Soul working in unison, you're not going to feel like you're working hard. In fact, you won't feel like you're working at all because your work is so much a part of you that it's inseparable from your life. This brings us to the idea of *success* and *freedom.*

Freedom

*Sometimes I do wake up in the mornings and
feel like I've just had the most incredible dream.
I've just dreamt my life.* – Sir Richard Branson

As he set off from Marrakech, Morocco in January, 1997,
attempting to circumnavigate the planet in his high-tech hot
air balloon, Sir Richard Branson was experiencing for the
many-thousandth time in his life the ultimate goal of true
entrepreneurs everywhere: freedom to do what you want to
do, when and how you want to do it.

Most of you are probably quite familiar with this Ultrapreneur
of Ultrapreneurs – the founder of the Virgin Group which
includes over 200 companies involved in every industry imagin-
able, from clothing and consumer electronics to environmen-
tally conscious fuels and space travel. It has been said – and I
think quite aptly – that "Richard Branson's life is better than
a fairy tale" (by Betsy Morris in her September, 2003 article,
"Richard Branson: What a Life", in *Fortune* magazine). From
the day he dropped out of school at age 16 – and I don't mean
to knock education by mentioning this – Branson has been
doing things according to his own vision, which comes from his
authentic self. His work is so authentic that he says he cannot
separate it from play. To him "it's all living."

When Branson isn't embarking on a new business venture of
some sort (including my favorite new one, Virgin Galactic,
which will give consumers rides into suborbital space), he's
attempting to break world records in boating and hot-air
balloon travel, acting in cameo roles in movies and on televi-
sion and entertaining family and friends on his own Caribbean

island. His vision has expanded to include environmental and humanitarian causes as well. Among his many efforts in these arenas, Branson helps fund a group called The Elders, which includes renowned humanitarians like Desmond Tutu and Jimmy Carter, and dedicates itself to finding peaceful resolutions to world conflicts and helping to ease human suffering.

You can bet that Branson loves what he does on a day-to-day, hour-to-hour, minute-to-minute basis. But the most important thing to understand is that money has never been his sole purpose; it hasn't even been his most important purpose. If it had been, he'd have retired a long time ago. He never intended to become a CEO, either, but understood that it was the only way to keep his original venture – a magazine that he published in the late 1960s – afloat. He learned early on how to keep things fun by having systems in place that worked in a natural way to keep his company organized. Branson keeps pursuing his passions and vision, which evolve along with his own personal growth and experience. Money has certainly been a fortunate byproduct of his vision, but the real success for him is having the freedom to pursue his heart's desire, whatever that may be on any given day.

Now, I'm not suggesting that Richard Branson's larger-than-life way of living is the only picture of success. As with everything else we've discussed so far, it's all about what's inside of you. I simply use Branson to illustrate the idea of success equaling freedom because he provides such a marvelous example of the sky being the limit when it comes to doing what you choose with your day. As you get closer and closer to running your business in a 100 percent authentic way, you'll enjoy increasingly greater freedom to use your time as you wish to use it. This is the true measure of a successful business. I can honestly say that I've reached the point in my business where I enjoy what I do all day long, and that I feel free to pursue whatever I want to pursue. It's an incredible feeling.

Branson likes to do things big – that's part of his authentic self – but for you, success might mean having the freedom to start a second business that compliments your first one, or to travel overseas to trace your ancestry, or perhaps to set up a program that positively impacts young people in your community. You're bound to discover new, seemingly different visions as you gain more freedom, and as long as they come from your authentic self, I encourage you to pursue them. Freedom is the goal of every entrepreneur, but how you decide to use it is entirely up to you. Remember: It's whatever *you* want to do, how and when *you* want to do it.

Author's note: Thank you for reading my book. I hope you enjoyed it and were able to get many useful things out of it. My hope is that you become as successful as you wish, and that you will do things for the good of everyone you are able to touch. Being an entrepreneur gives us incredible opportunities to help people without any restrictions. So think big, don't limit yourself, and ask "why" as much as you can. It is your intuitive, innovative, entrepreneurial spirit that has the ability to create the future. Stay true to yourself; be authentic in everything you do, and work in a way that is natural to you. It is the journey that is the message. Have fun with what you do day-to-day, hour-to-hour and minute-to-minute. Take care of yourself; you have a lot to create. This e-book will help you structure how to achieve all of the above. It is a roadmap. I hope I can be your guide.

Freedom

One More Thing

The only real valuable thing is intuition. - Albert Einstein

Most people that start their own business begin as "entrepreneurs" and they have all this excitement, energy, and passion and they sound like Tony Robbins. But after some time, they become overworked, overwhelmed, frustrated and they sound like the teacher in the movie Ferris Bueller... "Bueller, Bueller!" And they have become "business owners." These are the business owners that have a 95% failure rate. How does this happen? How do they go from energy and passion to frustration and failure?

Everything that they have done prior to starting their own business has not prepared them for being an entrepreneur. First, they go to school. School is a completed structure that includes orientation, training, rules and regulations, evaluations, teachers that tell them what to do, when to do it, and how to do it. Then, most of them go to work for someone before they start their own business. Working for someone else is very similar to school. There is an orientation, training, rules and regulations, evaluations, and a boss to tell them what to do, when to do it, and how to do it. It too is a completed structure.

Then they go into the entrepreneurial world. The entrepreneurial world isn't a completed structure. It's a work in process because there aren't enough resources to complete it when the business is started. Some owners may be able to borrow money; maybe have an SBA loan or something similar. But most of the time they borrow from the three "F's"; family, friends, and fools. Even if they are able to get an SBA loan or something similar it's not enough to create a completed structure. Therefore, all of the components schools and corporate America have, like systems, departments, manager, etc., do not exist. And there is no one to tell the new business owner what to do, when to do it, and how to do it. They therefore become reactors. They react to their clients or customers, their vendors, their employees, etc. and create a chaotic mess starting as an Egopreneur and continuing as an Entrepreneur.

This is how the entrepreneur gets into the mess they find themselves in. They have gone from the entrepreneur, being mainly on the right side of their brain, the creative side of their brain to become the business owner and being mostly on the left side of their brain. They have gone from the creative person, to the person tying to manage everything. In the process they have lost the creative side, the side that brought them the excitement and passion to start their business.

In this book we have looked at the Stages of entrepreneurial evolution; Egopreneur, Entrepreneur, and Ultrapreneur. Each of these stages let's you know where you are on your journey. The Egopreneur is the entrepreneur that starts the business but by the time they try to make the transition to become the Entrepreneur they are the business owner that is frustrated and about to fail.

We have also talked about the four steps to get you to where you want to go; Vision, Comfort Zones, Time, and Systems. And we have talked about the five elements; Understanding Business, Passionate Creation, Authenticity, Day-To-Day Happiness, and Your Market. Each of these help you maintain the vision that you have created.

But, One More Thing...

The biggest problem most entrepreneurs have is not knowing

what to do, when to do it, and how to do it on a daily, minute-to-minute basis in their business. In school and when working for someone else we are "trained" to learn one linear process after another. And as long as we do what we are told to do in the classroom or in our cubical, everything is OK. But things don't happen in the entrepreneurial world one linear process at a time. Many things are happening simultaneously. How do we know what to do, when to do it, and how to do it when things are flying all around us? How do we make decisions, and the right decisions when no one is there to tell us?

If we are going to make a decision or solve a problem, we have several choices. We can use the left side of our brain. The left side of the brain is the analyst, the one that figures out linear processes, systems, etc. and would be too slow to make the minute-to-minute decisions required. We could use the right side of our brain, but it's more concerned with creating what will be in the future. We could use our experience; but wait we don't have any. We could use our education; but that doesn't work in the entrepreneurial world. Or, we could use all of these and more.

The intuitive mind is a sacred gift and the rational mind is a faithful servant. We have created a society that honors the servant and has forgotten the gift. – Albert Einstein

Steve Job's quest for spiritual enlightenment took him to India in the summer of 1974. It was in India he learned the power of "intuition."

I have taken many years of intuition classes. In one class we were asked to listen to a cassette that played a person saying their name three times and then to be open to what came to us in the next five minutes of contemplation. We did not know who this person was or anything about them. When it was my turn to say what came to me, I said that this person had been in a confined place for some time, but now was not. Later we were told that this person had been in a coma for four years and had recently come out of it!

Where did that from? I don't know, but it was there and it was powerful! I believe all of us have intuition. It's that gut feeling that is never wrong. But we are not encouraged to use it. We talk ourselves out of trusting it and rationalizing something other than what out gut tells us. And then we say, "I knew that was going to happen!"

I encourage my clients to use their intuition. Be open to their gut feelings. To practice using it in their daily business decisions. It is very powerful and always works.

Here is an exercise you can do to develop your intuition. Get together with several people, preferably people you don't know that well, and have each of them exchange something that is personal to them. It could be something like a wallet or purse or something in their wallet or purse. Have everyone hold the exchanged object in their hands, close their eyes and take three deep breathes. Then just be open to what comes to you. Don't try to judge it or figure it out, just be open to it. After several minutes, open your eyes and tell the other person you received the object from, what came to you. You will be surprised at what happens!

Believe that things will work out somehow... follow your intuition and curiosity... trust your heart even when it leads you off the well-worn path... You have to trust that the dots will somehow connect in your future... The only way to do great work is to love what you do. If you haven't found it yet, keep looking. Don't settle. As with all matters of the heart, you'll know when you find it... Have the courage to follow your heart and intuition. They somehow already know what you truly want to become. Everything else is secondary.
– Steve Jobs, Apple

Worksheets

MY STORY WORKSHEET

As I did in the book, start to write down your life history. Start from the beginning and think about the significant events that occurred during your life. Ask yourself what impact these significant events had on you. For example, did they make you feel more or less empowered?

Did they point you in a different direction? After writing down as much as you can remember, see if you can notice any patterns. Is there a theme throughout? Do the dots connect? This exercise is to help you begin to notice the parts of you that make up your authentic self... to notice the things you "love" to do.

Answer the following questions about yourself. They will help you discover the things you did naturally before you started to be assimilated into society and were told what to do, how to do it, and when to do it. This exercise is to help you find parts of your authentic self.

1.) What did you like to do most when you were a child?

_____

_____.

2.) What toys did you play with?

_____.

3.) What are your favorite memories?

_____

_____.

4.) Who were your friends and what did they have in common?

_____

_____.

5.) What did you want to grow up to be?

_____.

VISION WORKSHEET

Answer the questions about your *vision*. Remember to include what you will be doing on a day-to-day, hour-to-hour, minute-to-minute basis. Think about how your answers will be connected to your authentic self.

What are you ultimately trying to create with the business? (Please prepare in bullet points).

-
-
-
-
-
-
-
-

What is the time frame to accomplish this?

_____

_____

_____

_____

_____

_____

Worksheets

Why are you trying to accomplish this?

_____

_____

_____

_____

_____

_____

How are you going to do this?

_____

_____

_____

_____

_____

_____

_____

VISION WORKSHEET

Answer the following questions with a "yes" or "no" to assess your commitment to your *vision*.

1.)   I know what my vision is.

2.)   I have no doubts that I will realize my vision.

3.)   I know that my vision when completed will be useful and worthwhile to others.

4.)   I will do whatever it takes to realize my vision.

5.)   I won't let anything stop me from realizing my vision.

Worksheets

COMFORT ZONES WORKSHEET

What five things must be completed in the next six months that are critical to my company's success?

1.)_____

_____

_____

2.)_____

_____

_____

3.)_____

_____

_____

4.)_____

_____

_____

5.)_____

_____

_____

TIME WORKSHEET

Write down the tasks you're bad at, good at, and love to do. Look at the tasks you are bad at. How can you start to move away from doing those tasks? Then start to look at the tasks that you are good at (but drain you). How can you start to move away from doing those tasks?

BAD   GOOD   LOVE

_____

_____

_____

_____

_____

_____

_____

_____

_____

_____

_____

_____

_____

Worksheets

TIME WORKSHEET

Decide that you are going to take control of your *time*. Start by making a commitment to yourself to start today and take 15 minutes to do something you love to do in your business. Schedule the next week so that you take 15 minutes each day to do something you love in your business. Schedule the next month. Schedule 30 to 60 minutes to do things you love to do in your business.

SYSTEMS WORKSHEET

Use the Business Needs Assessment to identify the weaknesses that exist in your business at present by completing the next 6 pages. Each section has 5 questions. The rating is from 1 to 5: 1 being a poor rating and 5 being an excellent rating. If, in any section, you score a total of 15 or below, you have identified a potential weakness that must be solved immediately.

Rate the following questions from 1 to 5
1 = very poor
2 = below average
3 = average
4 = above average
5 = excellent

MARKETING

Rate the company's current marketing plan. 1　2　3　4　5

Rate the company's implementation of current marketing plan. 1　2　3　4　5

Rate the company's ability to monitor the current marketing plan. 1　2　3　4　5

Rate the employee integration of the current marketing plan. 1　2　3　4　5

How does your marketing plan compare to the competition? 1　2　3　4　5

SALES

Rate the effectiveness of the company's sales force. 1　2　3　4　5

Rate the effectiveness of the company's sales training systems. 1　2　3　4　5

Rate the company's ability to monitor the achievements of sales goals. 1　2　3　4　5

Rate the company's ability to create incentives for its sales force. 1　2　3　4　5

Rate the company's ability to reach its sales goals. 1　2　3　4　5

CASH FLOW

Rate the company's overall cash management abilities. 1　2　3　4　5

Rate the company's system for managing cash flow. 1　2　3　4　5

Rate the abilities of person responsible for managing cash flow. 1　2　3　4　5

Rate the company's ability to borrow money when needed. 1 2 3 4 5

Rate the company's ability to manage accounts receivable and accounts payable. 1 2 3 4 5

PRODUCTION

Rate the effectiveness of the company's production management. 1 2 3 4 5

Rate the company's ability for production to meet sales goals. 1 2 3 4 5

Rate the effectiveness of company's inventory management. 1 2 3 4 5

Rate the company's ability to sell product for profitable price. 1 2 3 4 5

Rate the company's ability to fill backorders. 1 2 3 4 5

MANAGEMENT

Rate the company's management philosophy. 1 2 3 4 5

Rate the company's ability to fill management positions. 1 2 3 4 5

Rate the company's management training systems. 1 2 3 4 5

Rate the company's management integration with owners. 1 2 3 4 5

Rate the company's management integration with employees. 1 2 3 4 5

PRODUCT DEVELOPMENT

Rate the systems in place for product development. 1 2 3 4 5

Rate the product development budget effectiveness. 1 2 3 4 5

Rate the success of new products developed in the last three years. 1 2 3 4 5

Rate the competence of persons responsible for product development. 1 2 3 4 5

Rate the company's product development compared to competition. 1 2 3 4 5

LEADERSHIP/VISION

Rate the company's leadership effectiveness. 1 2 3 4 5

Rate the company's leader's ability to communicate to employees. 1 2 3 4 5

Rate the company's vision to the company's future success. 1 2 3 4 5

Rate the leader's ability to communicate the company's vision to employees. 1 2 3 4 5

Is the leadership style consistent? 1 2 3 4 5

COMPANY EVOLUTION

Rate the company owner's ability to delegate. 1 2 3 4 5

Rate the company owner's ability to manage. 1 2 3 4 5

Rate the company's effectiveness to be completely proactive. 1 2 3 4 5

Rate the company's image. 1 2 3 4 5

Rate the company's customer satisfaction. 1 2 3 4 5

SYSTEMS

Rate the company's accounting systems. 1 2 3 4 5

Rate the company's business management systems. 1 2 3 4 5

Rate the company's employee management systems. 1 2 3 4 5

Rate the company's tax planning systems. 1 2 3 4 5

Rate the company's cash flow systems. 1 2 3 4 5

BUSINESS PLAN

Rate the current business plan overall. 1 2 3 4 5

Rate the competence of the person responsible for developing the business plan. 1 2 3 4 5

Rate the company's ability to implement the business plan. 1 2 3 4 5

Rate the company's ability to monitor the business plan. 1 2 3 4 5

Rate the business plan compared to competition. 1 2 3 4 5

Worksheets

COMPANY CULTURE

Rate the company's culture as it corresponds to the company vision. 1 2 3 4 5

Rate the company's teamwork abilities. 1 2 3 4 5

Rate how the culture integrates throughout the company. 1 2 3 4 5

Rate the consistency of the company's culture. 1 2 3 4 5

Rate the company's culture compared to the competition. 1 2 3 4 5

COMPANY OWNERSHIP

Rate the company owner's ability to eventually sell the business. 1 2 3 4 5

Rate the owner's ability to attract new critical personnel. 1 2 3 4 5

Rate the owner's succession plan. 1 2 3 4 5

Rate the owner's ability to attract new investors. 1 2 3 4 5

Rate the owner's ability to grow with the company. 1 2 3 4 5

EMPLOYEE RELATIONS

Rate the company's overall employee relations. 1 2 3 4 5

Rate the company's relationship between employees and management. 1 2 3 4 5

Rate the company's relationship between employees and owners. 1 2 3 4 5

Rate how employees feel empowered in their job positions. 1 2 3 4 5

Rate how employees feel their input is taken seriously by the owners/managers. 1 2 3 4 5

COMPANY TRENDS

Rate the owner's ability to track company trends. 1 2 3 4 5

Rate the owner's ability to know which trends are critical. 1 2 3 4 5

Rate the owner's ability to react to negative trends. 1 2 3 4 5

Rate the owner's ability to communicate vital factors to employees. 1 2 3 4 5

Rate the owner's ability to control the company's vital factors. 1 2 3 4 5

COMPETITION

Rate the company compared to the competition. 1 2 3 4 5

Rate what your company offers employees compared to the competition. 1 2 3 4 5

Rate the company's ability to get new customers compared to the competition. 1 2 3 4 5

Rate the company's products/service compared to the competition. 1 2 3 4 5

Rate the company's ability to become more competitive. 1 2 3 4 5

SYSTEMS WORKSHEET

Identify the things that keep coming up over and over again that distract you from working on your goals and vision. Think about how you can create a *system* that will stop these things from being a distraction over and over again.

_____

_____

_____

_____

_____

_____

_____

_____

_____

_____

_____

_____

_____

_____

_____

_____

_____

_____

_____

_____

_____

_____

SYSTEMS WORKSHEET

Delegation:

When you decide to hire someone, begin to prepare a *system* for management and monitoring by asking the following questions:

1.)　What information do I need?

2.)　From whom?

3.)　By when?

You need to have the person you hire answer these questions in a format that is not verbal. The easiest format is to have a paper or electronic checklist.

These same questions can create an interactive system when you have hired more than one person.

The questions that each person answers will create the checklist for the others.

In other words, if you need certain information from someone by a certain time, part of his or her job description will be to prepare that certain information and to give it to you by the time you need it.

Recommendations

Books Nigel recommends:

1.) Mine, of course!

2.) The Velveteen Rabbit by Margery Williams

3.) The Wisdom of Florence Scovel Shinn by Florence Scovel Shinn

4.) The Four Agreements by Don Miguel Ruiz

5.) Anything by Deepak Chopra

Websites to visit:

www.UltrapreneurCoach.com

www.CoachFederation.com

About the Author

Nigel D. Clayton has been an Ultrapreneur for over twenty five years. He owns two businesses at the present time, including Ultrapreneur Coach, a professional business coaching firm specializing in transforming Egopreneurs and Entrepreneurs into Ultrapreneurs. Nigel is a Professional Certified Coach as designated by the International Coach Federation. A Colorado resident since 1976, Nigel loves hiking and fishing in the Rocky Mountains, and is an avid Broncos and Avalanche (NHL) fan. He has worked with many, many business owners from diverse industries throughout his career. He enjoys helping people accelerate toward their visions and quickly overcome the obstacles that prevent them from truly being happy and successful.

10906277R00065

Made in the USA
Charleston, SC
14 January 2012